YOU

BOOKS BY BISHOP SHEEN

The Armor of God

Calvary and the Mass

Children and Parents

Communism and the
Conscience of the West

The Cross and the Beatitudes

The Cross and the Crisis

A Declaration of Dependence

The Divine Romance

The Divine Verdict

The Eternal Galilean

For God and Country

Freedom under God

God and Intelligence

God and War

Guide to Contentment

Liberty, Equality and Fraternity

The Life of All Living

Lift Up Your Heart

Love One Another

Moods and Truths

The Moral Universe

The Mystical Body of Christ

Old Errors and New Labels

Peace of Soul

Philosophies at War

The Philosophy of Religion

The Philosophy of Science

The Prodigal World

The Rainbow of Sorrow

Religion Without God

The Rock Plunged Into Eternity

The Seven Capital Sins

The Seven Last Words

Seven Pillars of Peace

The Seven Virtues

Seven Words to the Cross

Those Mysterious Priests

Thoughts for Daily Living

Victory Over Vice

Walk with God

The Way of the Cross

Way to Happiness

Way to Inner Peace

Whence Come Wars

You

Visit our web site at
www.albahouse.org
(for orders www.stpauls.us)

or call 1-800-343-2522 (ALBA)
and request current catalog

YOU

FULTON J. SHEEN, PhD, DD

*Agrégé en Philosophie de L'Université de Louvain and
The Catholic University of America*

ST PAULS

Library of Congress Cataloging-in-Publication Data

Sheen, Fulton J. (Fulton John), 1895-1979.
    You / Fulton J. Sheen.
        p. cm.
    Originally published by Our Sunday Visitor, Huntington, Indiana
Eighteen addresses delivered in the nationwide *Catholic Hour*, produced
by the National Council of Catholic Men, in cooperation with the National
Broadcasting Co., from Dec. 3, 1944 through Apr. 1, 1945.
        ISBN 0-8189-0951-X
1. Spiritual life—Catholic Church.   I. Title.

BX2350.3 .S54 2003
248.4'82—dc21

                                        2002154158

Imprimatur:
✠ John Francis Noll
Bishop of Fort Wayne

ISBN-10: 0-8189-0951-X
ISBN-13: 978-0-8189-0951-1

This Alba House edition is produced by special arrangement with the
Estate of Fulton J. Sheen and the Society for the Propagation of the
Faith, 366 Fifth Avenue, New York, NY 10001. It has been revised to
incorporate a more recent and more recognizable translation of the
Scripture texts.

This book is published in the United States of America
by Alba House, the publishing arm of the Society of St. Paul,
an international religious congregation of priests and brothers
serving the Church through the communications media.

Printing Information:

Current Printing - first digit   2   3   4   5   6   7   8   9   10

Year of Current Printing - first year shown

                2009   2010   2011   2012   2013   2014   2015   2016

A special word of thanks to the
Fulton J. Sheen Society of Perth Western Australia, Inc.
for having encouraged the publication of this book
and provided us with the text of this fine work.

TABLE OF CONTENTS

Are You Happy?... 1

What Is God Like?... 9

What Are You Like?.. 17

How You Got That Way.. 25

Who Can Re-make You?....................................... 35

Is Religion Purely Individual?............................ 43

How You Are Re-made 51

Faith... 59

Hope 67

Charity 75

The Hell There Is... 83

The Value of Ignorance....................................... 91

The Secret of Sanctity 99

The Fellowship of Religion 109

Confidence in Victory.. 117

Religion Is a Quest 125

The Purpose of Life 133

Easter 141

Biblical Abbreviations

OLD TESTAMENT

Genesis	Gn	Nehemiah	Ne	Baruch	Ba
Exodus	Ex	Tobit	Tb	Ezekiel	Ezk
Leviticus	Lv	Judith	Jdt	Daniel	Dn
Numbers	Nb	Esther	Est	Hosea	Ho
Deuteronomy	Dt	1 Maccabees	1 M	Joel	Jl
Joshua	Jos	2 Maccabees	2 M	Amos	Am
Judges	Jg	Job	Jb	Obadiah	Ob
Ruth	Rt	Psalms	Ps	Jonah	Jon
1 Samuel	1 S	Proverbs	Pr	Micah	Mi
2 Samuel	2 S	Ecclesiastes	Ec	Nahum	Na
1 Kings	1 K	Song of Songs	Sg	Habakkuk	Hab
2 Kings	2 K	Wisdom	Ws	Zephaniah	Zp
1 Chronicles	1 Ch	Sirach	Si	Haggai	Hg
2 Chronicles	2 Ch	Isaiah	Is	Malachi	Ml
Ezra	Ezr	Jeremiah	Jr	Zechariah	Zc
		Lamentations	Lm		

NEW TESTAMENT

Matthew	Mt	Ephesians	Eph	Hebrews	Heb
Mark	Mk	Philippians	Ph	James	Jm
Luke	Lk	Colossians	Col	1 Peter	1 P
John	Jn	1 Thessalonians	1 Th	2 Peter	2 P
Acts	Ac	2 Thessalonians	2 Th	1 John	1 Jn
Romans	Rm	1 Timothy	1 Tm	2 John	2 Jn
1 Corinthians	1 Cor	2 Timothy	2 Tm	3 John	3 Jn
2 Corinthians	2 Cor	Titus	Tt	Jude	Jude
Galatians	Gal	Philemon	Phm	Revelation	Rv

YOU

ARE YOU HAPPY?

ADDRESS DELIVERED ON DECEMBER 3, 1944

Are you perfectly happy? Or are you still looking for happiness? There can be no doubt that at one time or another in your life you attained that which you believed would make you happy. When you got what you wanted, were you happy?

Do you remember when you were a child, how ardently you looked forward to Christmas? How happy you thought you would be, with your fill of cakes, your hands glutted with toys, and your eyes dancing with the lights on the tree!

Christmas came, and after you had eaten your fill, blown out the last Christmas candle, and played till your toys no longer amused, you climbed into your bed and said, in your own little heart of hearts, that somehow or other it did not quite come up to your expectations. And have you not lived that experience over a thousand times since? You looked forward to the joys of travel, but when your weary feet carried you home you admitted that the two happiest days were the day you left home and the day you got back.

Perhaps it was marriage you thought which would bring you perfect happiness. Even though it did bring a measure of happiness, you admit that you now take your companion's love for granted. One is never thirsty at the border of the well.

Perhaps it was wealth you wanted. You got it, and now you are afraid of losing it. "A golden bit does not make the better horse." Maybe it was a desire to be well-known that you craved. You did become well-known only to find that reputation is like a ball; as soon as it starts rolling, men begin to kick it around.

The fact is: you want to be perfectly happy, but you are not. Your life has been a series of disappointments, shocks, and disillusionments. How have you reacted to your disappointments? Either you became cynical or else you became religious. If you became cynical, you blamed things, rather than yourself. If you were married you said: "If I had another husband, or another wife, I would be happy." Or you said: "If I had another job…"; or, "If I visited another nightclub…"; or, "If I were in another city, I would be happy." In every instance, you made happiness extrinsic to yourself. No wonder you are never happy. You are chasing mirages until death overtakes you. But cynicism did not work, because in seeking pleasures you missed the joys of life. Pleasure is of the body; joy is of the mind and heart. Lobster Newburg gives pleasure to certain people, but not even the most avid lobster fans would ever say that it made them joyful. You can quickly become tired of pleasures, but you never tire of joys. A pleasure can be increased to a point where it ceases to be a pleasure; it may even begin to be a pain if carried beyond a certain point; for example, tickling or drinking. But the joy of a good conscience, or the joy of a First Communion, or the discovery of a truth, never turns to pain.

Furthermore, have you noticed that as your desire for pleasure increased, the satisfaction from the pleasure decreased? Do you think a philosophy of life is right that is based on the law of diminishing returns?

You think you are having a good time; but time really is the greatest obstacle in the world to happiness, not only because it makes you take pleasures successively, but also because you are never really happy until you are unconscious of the passing of time! The more you look at the clock, the less happy you are! The more you enjoy yourself, the less conscious you are of the passing of time. You say, "Time passed like everything." Maybe, therefore, your happiness has something to do with the eternal! The other reaction to disappointment is much more reasonable. It begins by asking: "Why am I disappointed?"; and then, "How can I avoid it?"

Why are you disappointed? Because of the tremendous disproportion between your desires and your realizations. Your soul has a certain infinity about it, because it is spiritual. But your body, like the world about you, is material, limited, "cabined, cribbed, confined." You can imagine a mountain of gold, but you will never see one. In like manner, you look forward to some earthly pleasure, or position, or state of life, and once you attain it you begin to feel the tremendous disproportion between the ideal you imagined and the reality you possess. Disappointment follows. Every earthly ideal is lost by being possessed. The more material your ideal, the greater the disappointment; the more spiritual it is, the less the disillusionment.

Having discovered why you are disappointed, you take the next step of trying to avoid disappointments entirely. You ask yourself: "What do I desire above all things?" You want perfect life, and perfect truth, and perfect love. Nothing short of the Infinite satisfies you, and to ask you to be satisfied with less would be to destroy your nature. You want life, not for two more years, but always; you want to know all truths, not the truths of economics alone, to the exclusion of history. You also want love without end. All the poetry of love is a cry, a moan, and a weeping. The more pure it is, the more it pleads; the more it is lifted above the earth, the more it laments.

With your feet on earth, you dream of heaven;

creature of time, you despise it; flower of a day, you seek to eternalize yourself. Why do you want Life, Truth, Love, unless you were made for them? How could you enjoy the fractions unless there were a whole? Where do they come from? Where is the source of light in the city street at noon? Not under autos, buses, nor the feet of trampling throngs, because their light is mingled with darkness. If you are to find the source of light you must go out to something that has no admixture of darkness or shadow, namely, to pure light, which is the sun. In like manner, if you are to find the source of Life, Truth, and Love, you must go out to a life that is not mingled with its shadow, death; to a Truth not mingled with its shadow, error; and to a Love not mingled with its shadow, hate. You go out to something that is Pure Life, Pure Truth, Pure Love, and that is the definition of God. And the reason you have been disappointed is because you have not yet found Him!

✝ It is God you are looking for. Your unhappiness is not due to your want of a fortune, or high position, or fame, or sufficient vitamins; it is due not to a want of something *outside* you, but to a want of something *inside* you. You cannot satisfy a soul with husks! If the sun could speak, it would say that it was happy when shining; if a pencil could speak it would say that it was happy when writing — for these were the purposes for which they were made. You were made for perfect happiness. That is your purpose. No wonder everything short of God disappoints you.

But have you noticed that when you realize you were made for Perfect Happiness, how much less disappointing the pleasures of earth become? You cease expecting to get silk purses out of sows' ears. Once you realize that God is your end, you are not disappointed, for you put no more hope in things than they can bear. You cease looking for first-rate joys where there are only tenth-rate pleasures.

You begin to see that friendship, the joys of marriage, the thrill of possession, the sunset and the evening star, masterpieces of art and music, the gold and silver of earth, the industries and the comforts of life, are all gifts of God. He dropped them on the roadway of life, to remind you that if these are so beautiful, then what must be Beauty! He intended them to be bridges to cross over to Him. After enjoying the good things of life you were to say: "If the spark of human love is so bright then what must be the Flame!"

Unfortunately, many become so enamored of the gifts the great Giver of Life has dropped on the roadway of life that they build their cities around the gift, and forget the Giver; and when the gifts, out of loyalty to their Maker, fail to give them perfect happiness, they rebel against God and become cynical and disillusioned.

Change your entire point of view! Life is not a mockery. Disappointments are merely markers on the road of life, saying: "Perfect happiness is not here." Though your *passions* may have been satisfied, *you* were never satisfied, because while your passions can find satisfaction in this world, you cannot. Start with your own insufficiency and begin a search for perfection. Begin with your own emptiness and seek Him who can fill it.

Look at your heart! It tells the story of why you were made. It is not perfect in shape and contour, like a Valentine Heart. There seems to be a small piece missing out of the side of every human heart. That may be to symbolize a piece that was torn out of the Heart of Christ which embraced all humanity on the Cross. But I think the real meaning is that when God made your human heart, He found it so good and so lovable that He kept a small sample of it in heaven. He sent the rest of it into this world to enjoy His gifts, and to use them as stepping stones back to Him, but to be ever mindful that you can never love anything in this world with your whole heart because you have not a whole heart with which to love. In order to love anyone with your whole heart, in order to be really peaceful, in order to be really wholehearted, you must go back again to God to recover the piece He has been keeping for you from all eternity!

WHAT IS GOD LIKE?

ADDRESS DELIVERED ON DECEMBER 10, 1944

How do you think of God?

Do you think of God as Someone on a throne who sulks and pouts and becomes angry if you do not worship and glorify Him and who is happy and grateful to you when you go to church and pray to Him?

Or do you think of God as a benevolent grandfather who is indifferent to what you do so long as you enjoy yourself?

If you hold either of these two views of God you cannot understand either why you should worship God, or how God can be good if He does not let you do as you please.

Let us start with the first difficulty: *Why worship God?*

The word "worship" is a contraction of "worthship." It is a manifestation of the worth in which we hold another person. When you applaud an actor on the stage, or a returning hero, you are "worshiping" him. Every time a man takes off his hat to a lady, he is "worshiping" her. Now to worship God means to acknowledge in some way His Worth, His Power, His Goodness, and His Truth.

If you do not worship God, you worship something, and nine times out of ten it will be yourself. If there is no God, then you are a god; and if you are a god and your own law and your own creator, then I am an atheist. The basic reason there is so little worship of God today is because man denies he is a creature. But we have not yet answered the question: "Why should you worship God?" You have a duty to worship God, not because He will be imperfect and unhappy if you do not, but because *you* will be imperfect and unhappy.

If you are a father, do you not like to receive a tiny little gift, such as a penny chocolate cigar, from your son? Why do you value it more than a box of Corona Coronas from your insurance agent? If you are a mother, does not your heart find a greater joy in a handful of yellow dandelions from your little daughter, than in a bouquet of roses from a dinner guest? Do these trivialities make you richer? Do you need them? Would you be imperfect without them? They are absolutely of no utility to you! And yet you love them. And why? Because by these gifts your children are "worshiping" you; they are acknowledging your love, your goodness, and by doing so they are perfecting themselves; that is, they are developing along the lines of love rather than hate, thankfulness rather than ingratitude, and therefore they are becoming more perfect children and happier children as well.

✝ As you do not need dandelions and chocolate cigars, neither does God need your worship. But if their giving is a sign of your worth in your children's eyes, then is not prayer, adoration, and worship a sign of God's worth in our eyes? And if you do not need your children's worship, why do you think God needs yours? But if the worship of your children is for *their* perfection, not yours, then may not your worship of God be not for His perfection, but yours? Worship is your opportunity to express devotion, dependence, and love, and in doing that you make yourself happy.

A lover does not give gifts to the beloved because she is poor; he gives gifts because she is already in his eyes possessed of all gifts. The more he loves, the poorer he thinks his gifts are. If he gave her a million, he would still think he had fallen short. If he gave everything, even that would not be enough. One of the reasons he takes price tags off his gifts is not because he is ashamed, but because he does not wish to establish a proportion between his gift and his love. His gifts do not make her more precious, but they make him less inadequate. By giving, he is no longer nothing. The gift is his perfection, not hers. Worship in like manner is our perfection, not God's.

God would still be perfectly happy if you never existed. God has no need of your love, for there is nothing in you, of and by yourself, which makes you lovable to God. Most of us are fortunate to have even a spark of affection from our fellow creatures. God does not love us for the same reason that we love others. We love others because of need and incompleteness. But God does not love us because He needs us. He loves us because He put some of His love in us. God does not love us because we are valuable; we are valuable because He loves us.

God thirsts for your love, not because you are His waters of everlasting life, but because you are the thirst, He the waters. He needs you only because you need Him. Without Him you are imperfect; but without you, He is still Perfect. It is the echo that needs the Voice, and not the Voice that needs the echo.

Now we come to that other misunderstanding concerning God which interprets His Goodness as indifference to justice, and regards Him less as a loving father than as a doting grandfather who likes to see His children amuse themselves even when they are breaking things, including His commandments.

Too many assume that God is good only when He gives us what we want. We are like children who think our parents do not love us because they do not give us revolvers, or because they make us go to school. In order to understand goodness, we must make a distinction between getting what we *want* and getting what we *need*. Is God good only when He gives us what we *want,* or is He good when He gives us what we *need* even though we do not want it? When the prodigal son left the father's house he said, "Give me." He judged his father's goodness by the way the father satisfied his *wants.* But when he returned a much wiser young man, he merely asked for what he *needed*: a restoration of his father's love; and hence he said: "Make me."

The thief on the left judged the goodness of Our Lord by His power to take him down from his cross; that is what he *wanted.* The thief on the right judged the goodness of Our Lord by His power to take him into Paradise; that is what he *needed.*

The Goodness of God means that God gives us what we *need* for our perfection, not what we *want* for our pleasure and sometimes for our destruction. As a sculptor, He sometimes applies the chisel to the marble of our imperfect selves and knocks off huge chunks of selfishness that His image may better stand revealed. Like a musician, whenever He finds the strings too loose on the violin of our personality, He tightens them even though it hurts, that we may better reveal our hidden harmonies. As the Supreme Lover of our soul He does care how we act and think and speak. What father does not want to be proud of his son? If the father speaks with authority now and then to his son, it is not because he is a dictator, but because he wants him to be a worthy son. So long as there is love, there is necessarily a desire for the perfecting of the beloved.

And that is precisely the way God's goodness manifests itself to us. God really *loves* us, and because He loves us He is not disinterested. He no more wants you to be unhappy than your own parents want you to be unhappy. God made you not for His happiness, but for yours, and to ask God to be satisfied with most of us as we really are is to ask that God cease to love.

Think of the thousands you have met whom you could never love. You may even wonder how their mothers could love them. But God loves them! He even loves them more than He loves *us* who look down on them with disdain and scorn.

If you want to know about God, there is only one way to do it: get down on your knees. You can make His acquaintance by investigation, but you can win His love only by loving. Arguments will tell you God exists, for God's existence can be confirmed by reason; but only by surrender will you come to know Him intimately.

That is one of the reasons why so many professors in secular institutions have no religion. They know about God, but they do not know God. And because they do not *love* what they already know, because they do not act on their belief, even the little they have is taken away. They rattle the milk cans of theology but they never drink the milk. Atheism is born from the womb of a bad conscience. Disbelief comes from sin, not from reason.

This is not a broadcast about God, it is a plea to love God. Worship Him because He is your perfection, more than knowledge is the perfection of the mind. Love Him because you cannot be happy without love. Love Him quite apart from all you are, for you have the right to love Him in your heart, even though you do not always succeed in loving Him in your acts. Think a little less about whether you deserve to be loved by Him; He loves you even though you are not deserving — it is His love alone that will make you deserving. It is love that confers value. "Nobody loves me" is the equivalent of being valueless. Hence the more important the person who loves you, the more precious is your value. You are infinitely precious because you are loved by God. Most of you are unhappy because you never give God a chance to love you. You are in love only with yourself. In the magnificent lines of Thompson, God may well ask you:

> "…Wherefore should any set thee love
> apart?
> Seeing none but I makes much of naught"

(He said),
"And human love needs human meriting:
    How has thou merited —
Of all man's clotted clay the dingiest clot?
    Alack, thou knowest not
How little worthy of any love thou art!
Whom wilt thou find to love ignoble thee,
    Save Me, save only Me?"

Say to yourself over and over again regardless of what happens: "God loves me!" And then add: "And I will try to love Him!"

WHAT ARE YOU LIKE?

ADDRESS DELIVERED ON DECEMBER 17, 1944

Thus far we have answered two questions: Why were you made, and what is God like? Now we ask: What are you like?

Take your heart into your hand as a kind of crucible and distill out of it its inmost nature. What do you find it to be? Are you not really a bundle of contradictions? Is there not a disparity between what you *ought* to do, and what you *actually* do? Do you not sometimes feel like a radio tuned in to two distinct stations, heaven and hell, getting neither, but only static and confusion worse confounded? The old Latin poet Ovid probably expressed your sentiments perfectly when he said: "I see and approve the better things of life, the worse things of life I follow." St. Paul too very likely expressed your inmost moods when he cried out: "Instead of doing the good that I want to do, I do the evil which I do not want to do" (Rm 7:19). You feel dual, divided against yourself, because you more often choose what you like, rather than what is best for you. And when you do, you always feel the worse for it. Somehow within you there is a "kink"; your human nature is disorganized. You feel frustrated; your realizations are anticlimaxes; they turn out to be the opposite of what you expected. You are a problem to yourself, not because of your more obvious faults, but because the better part of you so often goes wrong.

Your soul is the battlefield of a great civil war. The law of your members is fighting against the law of your mind. Your name is "legion" — you have no unifying purpose in life; there is only a succession of choices, but there is no one overall goal to which everything is subordinated. You are split into many worlds: eyes, ears, heart, body, and soul.

How explain this basic contradiction within you? There are four false explanations: psychological, biological, intellectual, economic.

The psychological explanation attributes this tension within you to something peculiar to you as an individual, your erotic impulses: As a child you were probably frightened by a mouse in a dark closet during a thunderstorm while reading a book on sex.

This hardly fits the facts because you are not the only one who is "that way"; everyone is. There is nothing queer about *you*. But there is something queer about *human nature*. Do you think that basically you are any different from anyone else in the world, or that you have a monopoly on temptations, or that you alone find it hard to be good, or that you alone suffer remorse when you do evil? It is human nature that is queer, not you.

The second false explanation is biological: that is, the kink in your nature is due to a flaw in evolution.

No! Evil is not due to the animal in you. Your human nature is very different from the animal's. There is a great discontinuity between a beast and a human. As Chesterton says: "You never have to dig very deep to find the record of a man drawing a picture of a monkey, but no one has yet dug deep enough to find the record of a monkey drawing the picture of a man."

An animal cannot sin, because it cannot rebel against its nature. He must follow it. But we can sin, because we merely ought to follow our nature. When you see a monkey acting crazily in a zoo, throwing banana peels at spectators, you never say: "Don't be a nut." But when you see a man acting unreasonably, you say: "Don't be a monkey." Man alone can be subhuman; he can sink to the level of a beast. The peculiar thing about a man is that though he may cease to act like a man, he never loses the imprint of human dignity. The divine image with which he was stamped is never destroyed; it is merely defaced. Such is the essence of man's tragedy. We did not evolve from the beast; we devolved to the beast. We did not rise from the animal level; we fall to the level of the animal. That is why unless the soul is saved, nothing is saved. Evil in us presupposes what it defaces. As we never, never can be godless without God, so we could never be inhuman without being human.

The third false explanation attributes the evil in you to want of education; you are perverse because you are ignorant. Once you are educated, you will be good.

No! You do not have this inner contradiction because you lack knowledge, for the educated are not all saints and the ignorant are not all devils. Enlightenment does not necessarily make you better. Never before in the history of the world was there so much education, and never before was there so little coming to the knowledge of the truth. Much of modern education is merely a rationalization of evil. It makes clever devils instead of stupid devils. The world is not in a muddle because of stupidity of the intellect, but because of perversity of the will. We know enough: It is our choices that are wrong.

Finally, the socialist explanation of this tension does not explain the facts; namely, people are wicked because they are poor.

Never before were living standards so high. All the poor are not wicked, and all the rich are not virtuous. If you had all the money in the world, you would still have that bias toward evil. If poverty were the cause of evil, why is it that juvenile delinquency increases in periods of prosperity and why does religion prosper in the vow of poverty? If poverty were the cause of evil, then riches should be the source of virtue. If that is so, why are not the wealthy the paragons of virtue? The world has not just made a few mistakes in bookkeeping which any expert accountant or economic adviser can correct; rather, the world has swindled the treasury of faith and morality. It is not the world's arithmetic that is incorrect; it is our morals that are bad.

Since this perversion of human nature is universal, that is, since it affects human nature (not just your personality exclusively or mine) it must be due to something that happened to human nature itself at its very origin; secondly, since it is not animal in its origin, but has all the earmarks of being deliberate and the result of a free choice, it must not be a part of God's original work, but must have come into being through some subsequent fault; thirdly, since evil is not merely a byproduct of bad environment but is endemic in the heart of man, it cannot be explained except on the basis of a universal fracture of some great moral law to which we are all bound. Some acts of disobedience can be remedied. If I throw a stone through a window, I can put in a new one. But there are other kinds of disobedience that are irremediable, for example, drinking poison.

Since evil is so universal in the world, it must be due to a disobedience of the second kind, which has affected us in our inmost nature.

An unequivocal voice in your moral consciousness tells you that your acts of wrongdoing are abnormal facts in your nature. They ought not to be. There is something wrong inside of us. God made us one way; in virtue of our freedom, we made ourselves another way. He wrote the drama; we changed the plot. You are not an animal that failed to evolve into a human; you are a human who rebelled against the Divine. If we are a riddle to ourselves, the blame is not to be put on God, but on us.

This being so, before you can be happy, you must throw overboard these three false notions which the nineteenth century put into your mind:

The first is the idea that you are naturally good and progressive, and — thanks to evolution, science, and inevitable progress — you are destined to become better and better until you become a kind of god. Two world wars in twenty-one years and the prospect of a third world war very soon knocks that false optimism into a cocked hat.

Discard also the idea that in order to come to God and religion, you must be good.

Finally, do not believe that religion consists only in moral platitudes and pious exhortations which cheer you up on the roadway of life regardless of the road you take.

In their place, start rebuilding your life with these three truths which alone do justice to your human nature.

Though you are not indefinitely progressive, neither are you a depraved criminal. You are not a saint, neither are you a devil. The tendency toward evil in you is not an irremediable flaw, but an accident that can be repaired. It is due to a bad choice and can be remedied by a right choice.

To come to religion, you need not be good. Rather you come to God because you are not good. If you were perfectly good, you would not need God. As Our Lord said: "Those who are healthy have no need of a physician..." (Mk 2:17).

You are right in not wanting a religion of moral platitudes. What you want is a religion of deliverance and redemption. Because of sin you feel like a fish on top of the Empire State Building; somehow or other you are outside of your environment.

HOW YOU GOT THAT WAY

Address Delivered on December 24, 1944

Anyone who gives freedom to another assumes great risks, whether it be a parent to a child or a Creator to a creature. In a certain sense, even God took a great risk when He made man free, for the very freedom to become a child of God implied the possibility of becoming a rebel.

Since God made us free to choose what is right, we are also free to choose the wrong. We too often interpret freedom as the right to break God's commandments. When you buy an automobile, the manufacturer will give you a set of instructions. He will tell you the pressure to which you ought to inflate your tires, the kind of oil your ought to use in the crankcase, and the proper fuel to put in the gas tank. Really, he has nothing against you because he gives you these instructions, as God had nothing against you in giving you His commandments. The manufacturer wants to be helpful: he is anxious that you get the maximum utility out of the car. And God is more anxious that you get the maximum happiness out of life. That is why He gives you commandments.

But of course you are free. You can do as you please. You *ought* to use gasoline in the tank, but you *can* put in Chanel No. 5. Now there is no doubt that it is nicer for your nostrils if you fill the tank with perfume rather than with gasoline. But the car simply will not run on Smell No. 5. In like manner we were made to run on the fuel of God's love and commandments, and we simply will not run on anything else. We just bog down. And that is what happened to human nature in the Fall.

God did not give man the frightening responsibilities of freedom without at the same time offering him incentives to choose right rather than wrong. God would not force His happiness on anyone. In almost so many words, God said to Adam and Eve at the very beginning of history: As an inducement to choose what is best, I shall give you certain gifts. If you use your freedom in the direction of what is best for you, that is, for your perfection, I shall give you permanently the supernatural gift of sharing in my Divine Nature, that is, of being a child of God and an heir of heaven. To this I add permanently some lesser gifts: You will never die, your passions will never rebel against your reason, and your mind will be free from error.

But to preserve these gifts for themselves and posterity, one condition was imposed on Adam and

Eve by God, and it was very easy. They merely had to love God who is their perfection. We must not think that this condition was equivalent to saying to a child: "If you eat a woolly worm, I will give you a dollar," because a woolly worm is not the perfection of a child. Rather, it was like saying to the child: "If you drink milk and eat good food you will be healthy." As obeying the laws of health is the perfection of the child, so too obeying the will of God is our perfection.

We said that the one condition imposed was that they love God. But how could man prove his love of God? How do you know anyone loves you? Because he tells you? Most certainly not! Love is proved only one way: by an act of choice, by choosing the one we love over something or somebody else. Love is not love unless it is free; it is only because of the possibility of saying "No" that there is so much harm in the "Yes."

Hence the choice presented to our first parents was between a fruit and a garden, the part and the whole. God said they could eat of all the fruits in the garden of Paradise, save the tree of knowledge of good and evil.

Was there anything unreasonable about the trial? Is not life filled with abundant instances of receiving rewards on the condition of love? Imagine a wealthy man going away for the summer and telling the chauffeur and his wife that they may live in his house, eat his food, drink his wine, use his cars, and ride his horses, but on one condition: That they must not eat the artificial apple he has on the dining room table. The owner well knows the artificial apple will give them indigestion. He does not tell them that. They ought to trust him in the light of all he has done for them. Now if the wife persuades her husband to eat the apple, she would not be a lady; and if he eats it, he would not be a gentlemen. By doing the one thing forbidden they would lose all the good things provided and have indigestion besides — and they even lose the opportunity of passing these things on to their children.

To make light of the fruit in the story of the Fall is to miss the point that it was the test of love. Not to shake hands with a passerby on the street is of no importance, but not to shake hands as a sign of contempt is very serious. Eating of the forbidden fruit was a sign of contempt; the symbol of rebellion. Like Pandora, man opened the forbidden box and lost all his treasures.

But you ask: Well! Granted that Adam sinned! What have I to do with Adam? Why should I be punished because of him? When President Roosevelt declared war on December 8, 1941, you declared war without any explicit declaration on your part. What the Chief of the Nation did, we did. Now Adam is the head of the human race. What he did, we did. "Through one man, sin entered the world" (Rm 5:12).

But you say: "It was very unjust of God to deprive me of friendship with Him, and these other gifts, simply because Adam sinned." There would have been injustice if God deprived you of your due. But you are no more entitled to be a child of God than a razor has a right to bloom, or a rose has the right to bark, or a dog has the right to quote Dante. What Adam lost was gifts, not a right.

On Christmas Day when you distribute gifts to your friends, would I have a right to say to you: "Why do you not give me a gift?" You would answer: "I am not doing you an injustice, because I owe you nothing. I am not even obliged to give these gifts to my friends. And if I had not given them gifts, I would not have deprived them of anything I owed them." So neither did God owe us anything beyond our nature as a creature of His handiwork.

But the loss of the supernatural gift of being a child of God weakened our will and darkened our intellect without corrupting our nature. The Fall disorganized our normal human faculties, making us just as we are now, with a bias toward evil, with a will reluctant to do good, with a tendency to rationalize evil. But each of us is still human — not a depraved human, totally corrupt, as those who ridicule the doctrine of the Fall say, but still a person capable of becoming what each once was. The disorder in us is like getting dirt in our eye: we still have the eye as an organ of sight, but it sees through tears. It is right here that Christianity begins. In all other religions you have to be good to come to God. In Christianity you do not. Because there is evil in the world, we need God. Christianity begins with the recognition that there is something in your life and in the world that *ought* not to be, that need not be, and that could be otherwise were it not for evil choices. If you are ever to be good, you must first believe you are bad.

If you know that you could be better than you are; if you feel like the master painting of a great artist that has become somewhat defaced and stained; if you know that though you are too good for the rubbish heap, you are nevertheless too spoiled to hang in the Metropolitan Gallery; if you know that you cannot restore yourself to your pristine beauty; if you know that no one could restore you better than the Divine Artist who made you — then you have already taken the first step toward peace. The Divine Artist did come to restore the original and He came on Christmas Day.

Such is the meaning of Christmas. The Son of God became man that man might become the adopted son of God.

This is Christmas Eve. Kind of sad, isn't it?

Fathers! Are not your sons away because

there is something wrong with the world? Then maybe God is out of His Heaven because there is something wrong with man. That star blazing in Bethlehem's sky is the Heavenly Father's service flag. His Son too has gone to war.

Mothers! You shrink in terror and fear from what might happen to your boy amidst whistling steel and whining shell. Then understand how another Mother drew a Babe to her breast in fear of the thundering hoofs and drawn swords of those who would take away His life before He had scarcely begun to live.

Sons and daughters in the service: To conquer, you must first make a landing in enemy territory. That was Bethlehem — God's beachhead in a land of sin. And how we must fight to keep it!

You dead on the far-thrown battlefields of the war! You died that others might live. You were the human expendables. This Babe is the Divine Expendable who came not to live but to die, that we might die to sin and live to love!

But you ask: how find Christmas peace in a world at war? You cannot find peace on the *outside* but you can find peace on the inside, by letting God do to your soul what Mary let Him do to her body, namely, let Christ be formed in you. As she cooked the meals in her Nazarene home, as she nursed her aged cousin, as she drew water at the well, as she prepared the meals of the village carpenter, as she knitted the seamless garment, as she kneaded the dough and swept the floor, she was conscious that Christ was in her; that she was a living ciborium, a monstrance of the Divine Eucharist, a Gate of Heaven through which a Creator would peer upon creation, a Tower of Ivory up whose chaste body He was to climb "to kiss upon her lips a mystic rose."

As He was physically formed in her, so He wills to be spiritually formed in you. If you knew He was seeing through your eyes, you would see in every fellow man a child of God. If you knew that He worked through your hands, they would bless all the day through. If you knew He spoke through your lips, then your speech, like Peter's, would betray that you had been with the Galilean. If you knew that He wants to use your mind, your will, your fingers, and your heart, how different you would be. If half the world did this there would be no war!

Why not resolve this year to spend an hour a day in His presence? Do not stay away because you are wicked. Remember that Babe did not come to earth because you are good, but because you are not. He did not come because there was Peace, but because there was none.

Children are so unsuspecting. Taking candy away from a baby is easy — but not as easy as taking happiness from that Child!

Let not your unworthiness keep you back. Remember, love is blind, and no love is as blind as this Child's; otherwise, how could He love you and me? He does love us and that is enough to make us very happy.

That is what I mean when from a devoted heart I say, "Merry Christmas, Friends!"

WHO CAN RE-MAKE YOU?

ADDRESS DELIVERED ON DECEMBER 31, 1944

A good way to start the new year is to ask how you can be different than you are now. Remember we said that we were like a clock whose mainspring was broken. We have the "works" but we do not "go." In order to put the clock in order, two conditions must be fulfilled: (1) The mainspring must be supplied from the outside, and (2) it must be placed inside the clock. Man cannot redeem himself any more than the clock can fix itself. If man is ever to be redeemed, redemption must: (1) Come from without human nature, and (2) be done from within.

Why must your salvation come from without? For the same reason that you cannot lift yourself by your own bootstraps. Human nature has contracted a bigger debt than it can pay. In sinning against God we piled up an infinite debt, and we have not enough balance of merits in our finite bank to meet the burden.

Furthermore, while you can destroy life you cannot create it; you can blind your vision but you cannot restore it; you can destroy your communion with God by sin but you cannot revive it. Evil is too deep-seated in the world to be righted by a little kindness or reason or tolerance. You might just as well tell a man suffering from gout that all he needed was to play six sets of tennis. Man has radically failed. He cannot save himself.

But though salvation must come from *without,* it nevertheless must be done from *within* humanity. It would do no good to the clock to put the mainspring inside a radio. If salvation were not done *inside* humanity, it would have no relation to humanity. If I were arrested for speeding, you could not go into the courtroom and say: "Try me instead of Father Sheen." The judge would say: "What have you to do with the case?" There is no substitution in the eyes of the law. Furthermore, any man who is conscious of his guilt does not want to be "let off." In our relations with our fellow man we often say: "I want to make up for it." There is no reason why, in our relation to God, we should act any differently. Hence human nature in some way must be involved in its own redemption.

To re-create fallen man in justice and mercy, Redemption must come from without and be accomplished within. Put both conditions together and the Redeemer was both God and man. If He were only man, He too would need Redemption; if He were only God He would have no relation to fallen man who needed Redemption. But if He were both God and man, then, as *man* He could act in our name; then, as *God* His Redemption would have an infinite value. This is what happened when God appeared in Bethlehem and took upon Himself our manhood as Jesus Christ. From that moment on, every word, every sigh, every breath, every tear, every heartache, and every pain of His human nature was the breath, the tear, the heartache, and the pain of the Person of God and therefore had infinite value.

If you want religion, keep in mind these three fundamental truths:

First, Jesus Christ is not just a good man. A good man never lies, but if Christ is not what He claimed to be — the Son of God — then He is the greatest liar of all times. A good man never deceives, but if Christ cannot give what He promised — that is, peace and pardon to our hungry tired souls — then He is the arch-deceiver of history. Either Christ is the Son of God or He is the anti-Christ — but He is not just a good man. Jesus Christ is both God and man. He was God before He was man. He is a God who became man, not a man who became God. He did not begin to be a Person at Bethlehem. From all eternity He is the Person of God. "In the beginning was the Word and the Word was with God, and the

Word was God.… And the Word was made flesh and dwelt among us" (Jn 1:14).

Second, Christ is the new Adam. The human race has two heads: Adam and Christ. Beneath all races, classes, and nations there are two humanities: the old, unregenerate humanity of Adam, comprised of all who are born of the flesh; and the new regenerated humanity of the new Adam, Christ, comprised of all who are born of the baptismal waters of the Holy Spirit.

The old human nature descended from Adam was infected by original sin. God would not take that upon Himself, because He would not put a patch of holiness on an old garment. The problem was now to be a man like us, without being contaminated as we were by sin! He could be a man like us, by being born of woman. He could be a sinless man, or the new Adam, by being born of a Virgin. By dispensing with an act of generation by which original sin was propagated, He escaped its infection. That is why He was born of a Virgin. The Virgin Birth broke the heritage of sin, as now for the first time since Adam there walked on earth a human nature as God meant it to be. Thus the three instruments which cooperated in the fall were reversed in redemption. For the disobedient Adam, there is the new obedient Adam, Christ. For the proud woman Eve, there is the humble Virgin

Mary. And for the tree of Eden, there is the new tree of the Cross on Calvary.

Third, Our Lord is not primarily a teacher of humanitarian ethics but essentially and primarily a Redeemer and a Savior. Everyone else came into this world to live; He came into it to die. Death was a stumbling block to Socrates; to Christ it was the goal of His life, the very gold He was seeking. Death in a certain sense was inevitable to Him, for once Love and Innocence confront brute force and sin, a crucifixion follows. Evil is always the form that love takes in an evil situation. Every mother who had an erring son, and every wife who ever had a drunken husband, knows that. How else could Divine Love meet sin, except by a cross? Suffering breaks some human hearts. Sin broke the heart of God.

How did this Redemption take place? *By the sinless Christ being made sin.* As doctors who are free from disease will sometimes permit themselves to be inoculated with a disease that they may find a cure, so He, though sinless, freely accepted the cumulative weight of human transgression that He might atone for the very punishment which our sins deserved. That is why His life is inseparable from the Cross. There are those who say the only reason Christ went to the Cross was to show us that He loved us, but not because we needed His Redemption. If you were sitting safely on a pier fishing and a good neighbor came up behind you, threw himself into the river and as he went down for the third time said, "This shows how much I love you," the whole ceremony would be ridiculous if it were not so tragic. But if you had actually fallen into the river, and the good neighbor lost his life saving you, then you could say of him truly: "Greater love than this no man has, that a man lay down his life for his friends" (Jn 15:13). It is through the Cross that Christ reconciles the world to God and restores to us those gifts which Adam lost in the fall.

It is something like this. Imagine a golden chalice which has been consecrated for divine worship and used on the altar at Mass. Suppose this chalice is stolen, mingled with alloys, and beaten down to a cigarette case. Later on it is recovered. Before the gold of that chalice can be restored to the altar, it must first of all be subjected to purging fires to burn away the dross. Finally it must be remolded by repeated blows of a hammer. Then only may it be readied for reconsecration and restored to its dignity and honor.

Our human nature was like that battered and desecrated chalice, no longer serving the high purpose for which it was made. The chalice could not remake itself. Neither could man redeem himself. So Christ took upon Himself our human nature and plunged it into the flaming furnace of Calvary's fires that the dross of sin might be burned away. Then on

Easter Sunday, by rising from the dead, He reversed the Fall and appeared as the New Man, remolded and glorified, fit for God's service and restored to God's friendship. But the Cross does not save us without our cooperation.

Christ has achieved the re-creation of man in His own person. Christianity consists in letting God do to your human nature something like unto that which He did to the human nature taken from His Mother. He is the beginning of a new coinage to take the place of the counterfeit. He is the original, the new die; millions and millions of worthy coins can be stamped from that die. Whether we do it and thus become regenerated depends on our will. Those of us who do it cease to be mere creatures; we begin to be, in the awful literalness of the phrase, an *adopted* son of God!

I beg you then to clean from your mind the contemporary rubbish that says you came from the beast. You did not come from the dogs, but you can go to the dogs. You are less a risen monkey than you are a fallen angel. You were once not lower than you are now, but you were once higher. You are more of a disinherited king than you are an enthroned beast.

The tragedy of life is not what people suffer, but how much they miss. They are living like animals when they ought to be living like children of God.

If you are willing to commit your life to Christ, this practical problem arises: How do you enter into a relationship with Him? What has He, who lived almost twenty centuries ago, to do with you? And what have you to do with Him? You probably often have seen painted on the rocks on the highways, signs reading: "Jesus Saves." Certainly He saves, but how? That question I shall answer next.

IS RELIGION PURELY INDIVIDUAL?

Address Delivered on January 7, 1945

Have you ever heard anyone say: "I do not want a Church standing between me and God"? This is like saying: "I do not want the United States Government standing between me and America." To say I want no one between God and me is anti-Christian because it implies that your brother is a barrier to God's grace and not a means to it. Did not Our Lord make love of God inseparable from love of neighbor? And did He not teach us to pray in the context of "Our Father," not "My Father"; "our daily bread" not "my daily bread"? And if God is a Father, then the others united to Him are brothers, and therefore our religion must be social.

You are not allowed an individual interpretation of the Constitution of the United States. A Supreme Court does that for you. Why, then, should you insist on an individual interpretation of religion and begin all religious discussions with: "*I feel* this way about God." "I feel." Never were the sublime and beautiful realities put so much at the mercy of a stomach. Do you have your own individual as-

-43-

tronomy and individual mathematics? Why, then, do you want your own individual religion?

You cannot practice religion alone any more than you can love alone. What would happen to your patriotism if you said, "Patriotism is an individual affair"? If you were the only person in a town, could you be charitable? If, then, you cannot be kind alone, or sacrificing alone, or generous alone, how in the name of God do you expect to be religious alone? As generosity implies a neighbor, as patriotism implies fellow citizens, so religion implies fellow men in relation to God. That brings us, then, to this important question we asked last week: How do you contact Christ the Redeemer? How do you come to know His Truth and His Will? Do you contact Him as an individual by reading about Him, by singing hymns to Him, or do you contact Him in fellowship and in community, the way that God Himself has ordained?

The way to answer that question is to inquire how mankind contacted God before the coming of Christ. Was religion a purely individual affair or was it corporate? Did God deal with individuals directly, or indirectly, that is, through a race, a society, or a community?

Search your Scriptures. And you will find that God always dealt with mankind through human corporations or races or moral bodies, presided over by a divinely appointed head. The Book of Genesis reveals that the history of mankind would be a warfare not between individuals, but between two seeds, two races, two corporate wholes: the power of darkness and the power of light.

Each corporation had a head. The head of the evil corporation was Satan; the invisible head of the corporation of good was God — but God always chose a visible head of that community to act in His name. First it was Noah through whom salvation would come to humanity. Very likely, at the time of the flood, every individual might have liked to have had his own personal row boat, but God saved them in an ark in His own way and under His own divinely appointed captain. Later there came new heads of this new spiritual corporation; such as Abraham, Isaac, Jacob, Moses, and others.

Whenever God willed to give a new or special privilege to this community, He changed the name of its head. That He did in the case of Abraham, and in the case of Jacob.

And so it came to pass that the most important word in the Old Testament was the word for this corporation, or body, or congregation, or society. And that word in Hebrew was *kahal*. Now about 200 years before Christ, the Jews translated their Scriptures into Greek. That was because so many Jews were living away from Israel in a Grecian civilization. When the translators came to the Jewish word *kahal*, they translated it by the Greek word, *ecclesia* — which means, "that which is called out," signifying that its members had been called out by God from the secular nations.

When finally God came to this earth in the person of Our Lord, it was only natural to expect that He would continue to deal with mankind in the same way that He had dealt with it before, namely, through a corporation presided over by a head whom He Himself would choose.

And, as once before He had named Abraham, Moses, and David as its head, so now He would name someone else as its head. And because new powers and privileges were to be given to the individual whom He would appoint as its visible head, as He changed Abram's name to *Abraham,* Jacob's name to *Israel,* so now He changed the name of the individual who is to be the new head of His *ecclesia* from Simon to *Rock.* In English, his name is Peter. But we lose the flavor of it in English because *Peter* and *Rock* are different words, but they are not different words in the language Our Lord spoke, nor are they different words, in the original Greek of the Gospel. And Our Lord said to this man: "Your name is Simon; henceforth, you shall be called the Rock." And on that day at Caesarea Philippi, when the Rock confessed that Christ was the Son of the Living God, the Divine Master said to him: "You are the Rock and upon this Rock, I will build my *ecclesia,* and the gates of hell shall not prevail against it." From now on God's *ecclesia* would be built upon the Rock and it would be to the whole world God's chosen community for the communication of His Divine Life, as Israel before had been the community for the giving of that promise. And through his new *ecclesia* or body Christ still teaches as He once taught through His own individual human nature. Therefore, the *ecclesia* must be infallible or free from error. It cannot be otherwise, for Christ is still teaching through His body: "He who hears you," He said, "hears me."

Through this *ecclesia* or body, Christ still governs. Therefore disobedience to His *ecclesia* would be a disobedience to Him, just as an insult to your body is an insult to your person. Through this *ecclesia* He still forgives sins. Therefore the publicans and the woman taken in sin have no advantage over you and me who live in this very hour.

And though this Truth and Power and Holiness are communicated through poor weak human natures in His *ecclesia,* that Truth and Power and Holiness cannot be spoiled any more than sunshine is polluted when it shines through a dirty window. Human nature in the *ecclesia* is only the instrument of the forgiveness and the truth. It is not the cause.

Are you surprised to hear that Christ acts through His Body or *ecclesia* today? Then recall the story of St. Paul who persecuted the *ecclesia* in the City of Damascus. Remember the heavens were opened, the glorified Christ now at the right hand of the Father roused that persecutor with the question: "Saul, Saul, why are you persecuting me" (Ac 22:7). Christ and the *ecclesia* — are they the same? Precisely. If someone steps on your foot, your head complains. Well, Paul was striking the Body of Christ: therefore the invisible head complained from Heaven.

And would it not be terrible if Christ could not prolong Himself through space and time? If He could not, how would He differ from Lincoln or Napoleon or Caesar? Do you think that God intended that the only ones who would know His Truth would be those who lived in His time? Was that Truth caught up by a Galilean breeze and wafted away, never to be known again? Shall we who live in the confusion of this twentieth century be without that Divine Light? Is forgiveness limited to Magdalens and to penitent thieves? Do you want His forgiveness now? I tell you that if Christianity is only the memory of someone who lived 1900 years ago, and who cannot communicate His Truth to you in this warring world of 1945, and who cannot absolve your sins this very night — if it cannot do these things, then Christianity is not worth preserving. Let us do away with it. If Christ is not the Eternal Contemporary, then He is not God.

You did not wait until you were twenty-one and then read the Constitution and the Declaration of Independence and decide to become an American. You were born out of the womb of America. And as you were born out of the womb of a political society, so as a Christian you were born out of the womb of Christ's society. You lived by it, before you knew it. It creates you spiritually by birth of the spirit, as your country created you by the birth of the flesh. The *ecclesia* is prior, both logically and chronologically, to its individual members. Though very few ever advert to it, this *ecclesia* was spread throughout the entire Roman Empire before a single book of the New Testament was written. It was the Bible that grew out of the *ecclesia,* not the *ecclesia* that grew out of the Bible.

Oh, I wish that I could tell you some of the joy of knowing that Christ lives and teaches and pardons and sanctifies in His *ecclesia* today; that just as He once taught and governed and sanctified through a human nature taken from Mary, over-shadowed by the Holy Spirit, so now He teaches, governs, and sanctifies through human natures in His *ecclesia,* overshadowed by the Pentecostal Spirit. When I kneel therefore before a priest in confession, I see Christ's absolving hand and hear the Voice that bid the sinner go and sin no more. When I see the Host and the chalice lifted up in Mass, I believe that Christ's commandment is fulfilled: "Do this in remembrance of me" (Lk 22:19), and I see Calvary projected through space and time to the very altar at which I kneel. When I see the *ecclesia* persecuted and mocked, I see Christ once more pelted with mud and spurned and spat upon and ridiculed, as I remember His words: "If the world hates you, know that it has hated me before you" (Jn 15:18). And as I hear that *ecclesia* articulate for me in an uncharted world the teachings of Christ, I am consoled, for what I want is a truth that is right not when the world is right, but a truth that is right when the world is wrong.

If ever you have an opportunity, when this war is over, to go to Rome, I want you to visit the tomb of that Rock, the fisherman. And when you have said your prayers there, lift up your eyes to that great dome — the greatest dome that was ever thrown against the vault of heaven's blue — and you will see inscribed upon it, in letters of gold, these words: "Tu es Petrus et supra hanc petram, aedificabo *ecclesiam meam*" — "You are the Rock and upon this Rock I will build my *ecclesia.*"

Ecclesia! — the very word the inspired Old Testament used to describe Israel as God's community; the very word the Son of God Himself used at Caesarea Philippi. And that *ecclesia* was built on Peter. Peter the Rock, who has lived through these 1900 years and in 252 distinct personages, and the name of that Rock today is the gloriously reigning Holy Father, Pius XII, the greatest moral authority in the world. I'm sorry. I should have told you long before this the meaning of the Greek word *ecclesia*. It means "the Church."

HOW YOU ARE RE-MADE

ADDRESS DELIVERED ON JANUARY 14, 1945

Have you ever thought that possibly there might be a higher life than the natural life you live now? I do not mean in the next world, but in this. Did you ever wish that you could know truths beyond your reason, that you could have reserves of power for crises, temptations, and sorrow over and above those you now possess, and that your soul could enjoy peace even in a world at war?

You have no right to say there is no higher life than the physical life you now live, any more than the rose has a right to say there is no life above it. You must remember that above the natural life which you live as a creature of God, there is such a thing as a supernatural life, which God gives to make you His adopted son. You have no strict right to this Divine Life. Just as it would be "super natural" or above the nature and powers of a rainbow to write poetry, or of a cow to quote Shakespeare, so in the strict sense it would be supernatural for you who are merely a creature of God's handiwork to be made a partaker of the Divine Nature and an heir of the Kingdom of God. Because that higher life is a free gift of God, it is called *grace*. Now in His goodness God has freely willed to restore to you the gifts and privileges of that life which were lost to you by the Fall, and this He does through the merits of Our Lord and Savior Jesus Christ.

If you thought about religion at all, you probably asked: But how can I contact that Divine Life of Christ who died over 1900 years ago?

The answer is: Christ would have to infuse His life into your soul. But how would it be done? Look at nature to see how a lower life is elevated to a higher life. How, for example, do the moisture, the carbons, and the phosphates in the earth ever live in the plant? First, the plant life must descend to them, take them up into its roots and branches, while the chemicals themselves must abandon the crude lifeless state they have in nature. If the plant could speak, it would say to the chemicals: "Unless you die to yourselves, you cannot live in my kingdom." Actually, the sunshine, chemicals, and moisture now begin to thrill with life and vitality in the plant. They have been, in the broad sense of the term, "super naturalized."

If the animal could speak, it would say to the plants: "Unless you die to your lower life of mere vegetation and submit yourselves momentarily to the jaws of death, you cannot live in my kingdom.

But once you live in me, you will share a life that not merely vegetates, but feels and moves and tastes and sees."

Man in his turn, going down to that which is lower, says to the animals: "Unless you die to yourselves by submitting to sacrificial death, you cannot live in my kingdom. But if you die to yourselves, you will share a life that is not merely sensible, but one that thinks and loves, has ideals, laughs and is artistic."

This is precisely what Christ says to you: "Unless you die to yourself, you cannot live in My Kingdom" — but with this difference: Since we are persons, which chemicals, plants and animals are not, the sacrifice enjoined on us is not physical, but spiritual. We do not have our personality destroyed, as a plant's nature is destroyed when taken into the beast. But otherwise the law holds good. The higher must come down to the lower; the Divine must descend into the human. Such was the Incarnation: God came down to man. But on the other hand, man must die to his sinful nature, his old Adam, his heritage of the Fall, and this he can do only by sacrifice, by taking up "his cross daily" and following Him. This is what Our Lord meant when He said: "If the grain of wheat that falls to the ground does not die, it remains alone. But if it dies, it bears much fruit" (Jn 12:24). The law of transformation holds sway: chemicals are lifted into plants, plants into animals, animals into man, and since man is free, he can will, through the Graciousness of God, to be lifted up into Christ, so that he can say: "I live, now not I; but Christ lives in me" (Gal 2:20). God came down to the level of man that He might in some way lift man to the level of God.

Now let us consider the normal ways in which that Life is communicated to us. Remember we said last week that the individual derives His life from the *ecclesia* or the Church; but the Church does not derive its life from the individual, as is the case with a club, a school, or a corporation. As no cell can live normally apart from your body, though your body can live without any individual cell, so you as a Christian cannot live a normal spiritual life apart from Christ's Body, the Church, but the Church can live without you.

Hence it is from the Church or Christ's Body that Christ's life pours out into your soul. And in order that the outpouring from that great Reservoir of merits on Calvary should not be haphazard, Our Lord instituted seven channels or Sacraments to convey that Life into your souls. Knowing that you have a body as well as a soul, He chose not to communicate His Divine Life to you invisibly. But since men are physical as well as spiritual, He willed normally to give you His supernatural life or grace under the symbol of some material sign. Thus by seeing water you would know something was being washed away, and by seeing bread you would know something was being nourished. Furthermore, by using these sensible signs for communicating His Spiritual Life, God restores the materials of a chaotic world back again into the divine order. How many Sacraments are there? There are seven and it is becoming that there should be seven, for there are seven conditions of life, physical and spiritual. Five of these refer to the individual life of man, and two refer to his social life.

1. As you cannot live a natural life unless you are born, so neither can you live the Christ-life unless you are born to it. That is why the Sacrament of Baptism is necessary for salvation.

2. As your natural life must grow to maturity and assume responsibilities, so you cannot lead a perfect supernatural life unless you mature in the Spirit and grow into the full responsibilities of being a Christian soldier. This is the Sacrament of Confirmation.

3. As you cannot live a natural life unless you nourish yourself, so you cannot lead a supernatural life unless you nourish the Divine Life which is already within you. This is the Holy Eucharist.

4. When you wound your natural life you must be healed; when you wound your supernatural life by sin you must be absolved, and that is the Sacrament of Penance, or Confession.

5. If your natural life suffers from a disease, the traces of that disease must be banished. Since no disease ever leaves traces comparable to the disease of sin, it follows that before meeting your God the remains of sin must be blotted out. That is the Sacrament of the Anointing of the Sick or Extreme Unction.

But you are not mere individuals in religion. You are members of the Body of Christ. In order that this spiritual corporation may perfect itself, and grow, two more conditions must be fulfilled.

6. As the natural life is preserved by propagation of the human species, so the supernatural life of the Kingdom of God is perfected by raising children of God. That is the Sacrament of Matrimony.

7. Finally, as your natural life must be lived under law and government, so your supernatural life must be lived under spiritual government, and this is the Sacrament of Holy Orders by which Christ's priesthood is prolonged to apply the fruits of law and order to all the members of His Mystical Body.

Christianity is not a system of ethics; it is a life. It is not good advice, it is Divine adoption. Being a Christian does not consist in being kind to the poor, generous to relief agencies, just to employees, gentle to cripples, though it includes all of these. It is first and foremost a *love relationship,* and as you can never become a member of a family by doing generous deeds, but only by being born into it out of love, so you can never become a Christian by doing good things but only by being born to it through Divine Love. *Doing* good things to a man does not make you his son, but *being* a son does make you do good things. Christianity begins with *being,* not with *doing,* with life and not with action. If you have the life of a plant, you will bloom like a plant; if you have the life of a monkey, you will act like a monkey; if you have the life of a man, you will do the things a man does; but if you have the Life of Christ in you, you will act like a Christian. You are like your parents because you partake of their nature; you are like God if you partake of His Nature. What a man does is the externalization of what he *is.*

Let me show you the difference: Most people have their actions governed by their background; for example, you think a certain way in order to defend your class or your wealth or your want of it; you do certain things because they are profitable or pleasant to you; you hate certain people because they are a reproach to your conscience or because they challenge your egotism. Your psychophysical make-up is the center of your life and therefore of your actions. You are, in a word, self-determined. Now to be a Christian means to discard self as the supreme determinant of actions; it means to put on the mind of Christ so as to be governed by

Christ's Truths, to surrender your will to His Will, and to do all things that are pleasing to Him, not to you. In other words, your life instead of being self-determined is Christ-determined.

How often we hear non-Christian men say: "Oh, you can do nothing with him. You can't make a silk purse out of a sow's ear." But the Christian answers: *"You can!* If God's grace ever gets into that man's soul, he will become a new creature."

You then who are Christians, who know that the Divine Life is in your soul, be conscious that your every word, thought, and deed is enacted before a Divine Audience. Let the Christ be the Unseen Guest at your every meal; your Divine Host in every visit; your Captain in every war; your Fellow-Worker in every task; your Father in every home; your Giver of every gift; the Listener in your conversation; your Companion in every walk; your Visitor at every knock; your Neighbor in every street; your Owner of every treasure; and your Lover in every love.

Do not fear God with a servile fear, for perfect love casts out such fear. Be bold enough then to believe that God is on your side, even when you forget to be on His. Live your life not by law, but by love. As St. Augustine put it: "Love God and then do whatever you please." For if you love God, you will never do anything to hurt Him or break off relationship with Him — and then you will always be happy.

FAITH

ADDRESS DELIVERED ON JANUARY 21, 1945

Have you ever noticed the tremendous disparity of points of view between those who possess Divine Faith and those who have it not? Have you ever observed when discussing important subjects, such as pain, sorrow, sin, death, marriage, children, education, that the point of view of faith is now poles apart from what is called the modern view? It was not so many years ago that those who rejected many Christian truths were considered off the reservation; for example, the divorced who remarried, the atheists, the enemies of the family, and so forth. But today it is those with faith who are considered off the reservation. It is the others who are on it.

Why this difference in point of view between those who have the faith, and those who have it not? It is due to the fact that a soul in the state of grace has its intellect illumined, which enables it to perceive new truths beyond reason.

You have exactly the same eyes at night as you have in the day, but you cannot see at night, because you lack the additional light of the sun. So too, let two minds with identically the same education and the same mental capacities look on a Host enthroned on an altar. The one sees bread, the other sees Christ — not, of course, with the eyes of the flesh, but with the eyes of faith. Let them both look on death: one sees the end of a biological entity, the other an immortal creature being judged by God on how it used its freedom. The reason for the difference is: One has a light which the other lacks, namely, the light of faith.

What then is faith? Faith is not believing that something will happen, nor is it the acceptance of what is contrary to reason, nor is it an intellectual recognition which a man might give to something he does not understand or which his reason cannot prove, for example, relativity. Rather, faith is the acceptance of a truth on the authority of God revealing. Assisted by the grace of God, we believe as true those things which He revealed, not because the truth of these things is clearly evident from reason alone, but because of the authority of God, who cannot deceive nor be deceived.

You believe not because of the arguments; they were only a necessary preliminary. You believe because God said it. The torch now burns by its own brilliance.

Would you like to know four things which faith will do for you?

1. *It will perfect your reason.* Faith is to your reason what a telescope is to your eye. It opens vaster fields of vision and new worlds, which before were hidden and unknown. As reason is the perfection of the senses, so faith is the perfection of reason. (Incidentally, reason alone will not get us out of the mess we are in today, because reason unaided cannot function well enough to handle the problems created by sin, by loss of faith, and by misuse of reason.)

Faith is not a dam which prevents the flow of the river of thought; it is a levee which prevents unreason from overflowing the countryside of sanity. Faith will enlarge your knowledge, because there are so many truths beyond the power of reason. You can tell something of the skill, the power, the technique of an artist by looking at his painting, but you could never know his inmost thoughts unless he revealed them to you. In like manner, you can know something of the Power and Wisdom of God by looking at His universe, but you could never know His Thoughts unless He told you. And the telling of the inner life is Revelation, which we know by faith. Without faith many minds are like flattened Japanese lanterns, a riot of color without pattern or purpose, a conglomeration of bits of information, but with no unifying philosophy of life. What a candle on the inside of the lantern will do to its pattern, that faith will do for your reason, that is, converge all your different pieces of knowledge into one absorbing philosophy of life which leads to God. That incidentally is why faith does not necessarily require an education. *Faith is an education.* God is our Teacher. That is why a little child in the first grade who knows God made him and that he is made for God is far wiser than a university professor who can explain an atom, but does not know why he is here or where he is going.

Unless you know why you are living, there is not much purpose in living.

2. *Faith will perfect your freedom.* Our Divine Lord said: "...the truth shall make you free" (Jn 8:32). If you know the truth about an airplane, you are free to fly it; if you know the truth about a triangle, that it has three sides, you are free to draw it. Try to be "broad-minded" and give a square five sides instead of four, as they did in the Dark Ages, and see where you end. Turning the words of Our Lord around, they mean that if you do not know the truth you will be enslaved. That is why, as the world denies Absolute Truth and Righteousness, it becomes enslaved. Socialism, for example, is nothing but the compulsory organization of a chaos created by the repudiation of Truth and Morality. Never, therefore, believe that you lose your freedom by accepting the Faith.

A few years ago, I received a letter from a radio listener who said: "I imagine that you from your earliest youth were surrounded by priests and nuns who never permitted you to think for yourself. Why not throw off the yoke of Rome and begin to be free."

I answered him thus: "In the center of a sea was an island on which children played and danced and sang. Around that island were great high walls which had stood for centuries. One day some strange men came to the island in individual row boats, and said to the children: 'Who put up those walls? Can you not see that they are destroying your freedom? Tear them down!' The children tore them down! Now if you go there, you will find all the children huddled together in the center of the island, afraid to play, afraid to sing, afraid to dance — afraid of falling into the sea."

Oh! how right was Our Lord. It is the truth that makes us free.

3. *Faith assures equality to all men* as children of God. Have you not noticed, if you have worked for or with a person of deep faith in Christ, that you have always been treated with gentleness, equality, and charity? You can not point to a single person who truly loves God who is mean to his fellow man. A man who does not believe in God will soon cease to believe in man.

In vain will the world seek for equality until it has seen men through the eyes of faith. Faith teaches that all men, however poor, or ignorant, or crippled, however maimed, ugly, or degraded they may be, all bear within themselves the image of God, and have been bought by the precious blood of Jesus Christ. As this truth is forgotten, men are valued only because of what they can *do,* not because of what they *are.* And since men cannot *do* things equally well — for example, play violins, fly planes, teach philosophy, or stoke an engine — they are and must remain forever unequal. From the Christian point of view, all may not have the same right to do certain jobs, because they lack the capacity — for example, Toscanini has not a right to pitch for the New York Yankees — but all men have the right to a decent, purposeful, and comfortable life in the structure of the community for which God has fitted them, and first and foremost of all, because of what they are: persons made to the image and likeness of God.

The false idea of the superiority of certain races and classes is due to the forgetfulness of the spiritual foundations of equality. We of the Western world have been rightly proud of the fact that we have a civilization superior to others. But we have given the wrong reason for that superiority. We assume that we are superior because we are white. We are not. We are superior because we are Christian. The moment we cease to be Christian we will revert to the barbarism from which we came. In like manner, if the black and brown and yellow races of the world become converted to Christ, they will produce a civilization and culture which will surpass ours if we forget Him who truly made us great. It is conceivable, if we could project ourselves a thousand years in the future, and then look back in retrospect over those thousand years, that we might see in China the record of a Christian civilization which would make us forget Notre Dame and Chartres.

4. *Finally, faith will give you peace of soul.* In the multitudinous duties of modern life you will do nothing which you cannot offer to God as a prayer; your sense of values will change; you will think less of what you can store away, and more about what you can take with you when you die; your rebellious moods will give way to resignation; your tendency to discouragement, which is due to pride, will become an additional reason for throwing yourself, like a wounded child, into the Father's loving arms; you will think of God's love as an unalterable dedication to goodness, to which you submit even when it hurts.

If you are sick you will see Christ's pierced hand laid upon you, and offer your sickness for your own sins and the sins of the world.

If your heart has been broken by infidelity, you will unite your loneliness with the Master who was deserted by His disciples who walked with Him no more.

If you are the victim of another's sin, then like the young woman who wrote me, the tragedy will be suffered through life for the redemption of the one who caused her ruin.

If your son is away in service, you will follow him, not by letter alone, but by prayer, as you both find a common center in God.

If you lost your boy in war, then you who spared not a son to save a world from tyranny, will be solaced by the Heavenly Father who spared not His Son to redeem a world from sin.

What a joy it was to one mother last week, who, receiving the personal effects of her boy who was killed in battle, discovered that in his pocket was a copy of *The Shield of Faith*, which we gave away last year on the air; and in that book there was underlined by the boy just one sentence which seemed so prophetic, "I am still in the eyes of God a person with an immortal destiny."

Faith will not explain why these tragedies happen, for if it did where would be room for the merit of faith? But it does give you the insight and strength to bear them. Anything in life can be borne if there is someone you love. The reason we are at war is because there are not enough people in love — with God.

HOPE

ADDRESS DELIVERED ON JANUARY 28, 1945

It is not so much what happens in your life that matters; it is rather how you react to it. You can always tell the character of a person by the size of the things that make him mad. A man can work joyfully at a picture puzzle, so long as he believes the puzzle can be put together into a composite whole. But if the puzzle is a hoax, or if it was not made by a rational mind, then one would go mad trying to work it out. It is this absence of purpose in life, along with its consequent fear and frustration, which has sometimes produced the neuroses and psychoses of the modern mind.

How do you react to the vicissitudes of life? Do you rebel because God does not answer your prayers to become rich? Do you deny God because He called away your husband, your wife, your child? In the midst of a war do you summon God to judgment as the criminal who started it all and ask, "Why does He not stop it?"

May I offer you three considerations to help

you build a firm hope in God?

1. *Remember that everything that happens has been foreseen and known by God from all eternity, and is either willed by Him, or at least permitted.*

God's knowledge does not grow as ours does, from ignorance to wisdom. The Fall did not catch God napping. God is science, but He is not a scientist: God knows all, but He learns nothing from experience. He does not look on you from heaven as you look down on an ant-hill, seeing you going in and out of your house, walking to work, and then telling an angel-secretary to note down the unkind word you said to the grocery boy. Why is it we always think of God as watching the bad things we do and never the good deeds? God does not keep a record of your deeds. You do your own bookkeeping. Your conscience takes your own dictation. God knows all things not by looking at you, but by looking into Himself as the Cause of all things. He never reads over your shoulder. An architect can tell you how many rooms will be in your house, and the exact size of each, before the house is built, because he is the cause of the becoming of that house. God is the cause of the *being* of all things. He knows all before they happen. As a motion picture reel contains the whole story before it is thrown upon the screen, so God knows all before it is acted on the stage of history.

But do not think that because God knows all, therefore He has predetermined you to heaven or hell independently of your merits and irrespective of your freedom.

His knowledge that you shall act in a particular manner is not the immediate cause of your acting, any more than your knowledge that you are sitting down caused you to sit down or prevents you from getting up if you willed to do it. Our Blessed Mother could have refused the dignity of becoming the Mother of God, as Judas could have resisted the temptation to betray. The fact that God knew what each would do did *not* make them act the way they did.

Because there is no future in God, *foreknowing is not forecausing.* You may know the stock market very well and, in virtue of your superior wisdom, foretell that such and such a stock will sell for 50 points in three months. In three months it does reach 50 points. Did you *cause* it to reach 50 points, or did you merely foreknow it? You may be in a tower where *you* can see a man advancing in the distance who has never been over that terrain before. You know that before he reaches the bower he must cross that ditch, wade that pond, tramp those bushes, and climb that hill. You *foresee* all the possibilities, but you do not *cause* him to cross those obstacles.

The following story illustrates the fallacy of

predestination without freedom. In the colonial days of our country there was a wife who believed in a peculiar kind of predestination, which left no room for human freedom. Her husband, who did not share her eccentricities, one day left for the market. He came back after a few minutes saying he forgot his gun. She said: "You are either predestined to be shot by an Indian, or you are not predestined to be shot. If you are predestined to be shot, the gun will do you no good. If you are not predestined to be shot, you will not need it. Therefore do not take your gun." But he answered: "Suppose I am predestined to be shot by an Indian on condition I do not have my gun?" And that was sound religion. It allows for human freedom. We are our own creators. To those who ask: "If God knew I would lose my soul, why did He make me?" the answer is: "God did not make you as a lost soul. You make yourself." The universe is moral and therefore conditional: "Behold I stand at the door and knock." God knocks! He breaks down no doors. The latch is on our side — not God's.

2. *God allows or permits evil but always for the reason of a greater good related to His love and the salvation of our souls.*

God does permit evil. Our Lord told Judas: "This is your hour" (Lk 22:53). Evil does have its hour. All that it can do within that hour is to put out the lights of the world. But God has His day. The evil of the world is inseparable from human freedom, and hence the cost of destroying the world's evil or stopping this war would be the destruction of human freedom. Certainly none of us wants to pay that high a price, particularly since God would never permit evil unless He could draw some good from it.

God can draw good out of evil because while the power of doing evil is ours, the effects of our evil deeds are outside of our control and therefore in the hands of God. The brethren of Joseph were free to toss him into a well, but from that point on Joseph was in God's hands. Rightly did he say to his brothers: "You thought evil against me: but God turned it into good..." (Gn 50:20).

The evil which God permits must not be judged by its immediate effects, but rather by its ultimate effects. When you go to a theater you do not walk out because you see a good man suffering in the first act. You give the dramatist credit for a plot. Why can you not do that much with God? The mouse in the piano cannot understand why anyone should disturb his gnawing at the keys by making weird sounds. Much less can our puny minds grasp the plan of God. The slaughter of the Innocents probably saved many boys from growing up into men who on Good Friday would have shouted, "Crucify Him." The physician would not permit an operation if he could not draw health from it, and God would not permit evil unless He could draw good from it.

3. *We must do everything within our power to fulfill God's will as it is made known to us by His Mystical Body, the commandments, and our lawfully constituted superiors, and we must also fulfill our duties flowing from our state of life. But everything that is outside our power, we must abandon and surrender to His Holy will.*

Notice the distinction between *within our power,* and *outside our power.* There is to be no fatalism. Some things are under our control. We are not to be like the man who perilously walked the railing of a ship in a storm at sea saying: "I am a fatalist! I believe that when your time comes, there is nothing you can do about it." What is wrong in fatalism is its failure to recognize that, within certain limits, our will *can* affect the events of life. It would be wrong for us, then, not to do our very best to make that course one which does good to our neighbor and renders glory to God. It is God's will that men should have a free will which they can use in subordination to His and thereby be happy. There was much wisdom in the preacher who said: "You run up against a brick wall every now and then during life. If God wants you to go through that wall, it is up to God to make the hole."

But we are here concerned with those things *outside our power,* for example, sickness, accidents, bumps on buses, trampled toes in subways, the barbed word of a fellow-worker, rain on picnic days, the death of Aunt Ellen on your wedding day, colds on vacation, the loss of your purse, and moth holes in your suit. God could have prevented any of these things. He could have stopped your headache, prevented a bullet from hitting your boy, forestalled cramps during a swim, and killed the germ that laid you low. But if He did not, it was for a superior reason. Therefore say: "God's will be done."

If you tell an Irishman it is a bad day, nine times out of ten he will answer: "It's a good day to save your soul."

It is one of the paradoxes of creation that you gain control by submission.

Does not the scientist gain control over nature by humbly sitting down before the facts of nature and being docile to its teachings? In like manner, surrender yourself to God, and all is yours. Even the irritations of life can be made stepping stones to salvation. An oyster develops a pearl because a grain of sand irritates it. Cease complaining about your pains and aches. When anyone asks, "How are you?" remember it is not a question, it is a greeting. An act of thanksgiving when things go against our will means more than a thousand acts of thanksgiving when things go according to our will.

Every person in the world is possessed: some are possessed by the devil, some are possessed by self, others are possessed by God.

This broadcast is an appeal to give your heart to God as if it were yours no longer, for your will is yours only to make it His. Pray not to change God's will; pray rather to change your own. Measure not God's Goodness by His readiness to do your will.

Shall we call Him "Father" and still not believe He wills what is best for His children? Think not that you could do more good for souls if you were well, or if you had another position. What matters in life is not where we are but whether we are doing God's will.

Trust not in God because you are good, but because He is good and you are not. Often during the day say: "God loves me, and He is on my side, *by* my side."

In wartime, do not ask: "If the Japanese and the English, the Germans and the Americans, pray to God; on whose side is God?" For the answer to this question is: "If we all prayed as we ought, we would all be on the same side: 'Thy will be done on earth as it is in heaven.'"

Neither ask: "Why do nations which love God fight one another?" The answer is: "They don't." You see how important is the love of God.

CHARITY

ADDRESS DELIVERED ON FEBRUARY 4, 1945

America's greatest enemy is not from without, but from within, and that enemy is hate: hatred of races, peoples, classes, and religions. If America ever dies, it will not be through conquest, but suicide.

Tolerance pleas will not remedy this hate, for why should any creature on God's earth be merely tolerated? There is more tragedy than we suspect in the fact that we have become most united as a nation at a moment when we have developed a hate against certain foreign countries.

Hate can be eradicated only by creating a new focus, and that is possible only by charity. By charity we do not mean kindness, philanthropy, generosity, or big-heartedness, but a supernatural gift of God by which we are enabled to love Him above all things for His own sake alone, and in that love, to love all that He loves.

The first quality of charity to be noted is that it resides in the *will,* not in the emotions or passions or senses. In other words, charity does not mean to like, but to love. Liking is in the feelings or emotions; loving is in the will. A little boy cannot help disliking spinach, as perhaps you cannot help disliking sauerkraut, and I cannot help disliking chicken. The same is true of your reactions to certain people. You cannot help feeling an emotional reaction against the egotistical, the sophisticated, and the loud, or those who run for first seats, or those who snore in their sleep.

But though you cannot *like* everyone because you have no control over your physiological reactions, you can *love* everyone in the divine sense, for love, being in the will, can be commanded. As Our Lord said: "A new commandment I give you: that you love one another, as I have loved you" (Jn 18:84).

Outwardly, your neighbor may be very unlikable; but inwardly he is one in whom the image of God can be recreated by the kiss of charity. You can *like* only those who like you, but you can *love* those who dislike you. You can go through life liking those who like you without the love of God. Humanism is sufficient for those of our set, or for those who like to go slumming from ivory towers, but it is not enough to make us love those who apparently are not worth loving. To will to be kind when the emotion is unkind, requires a stronger dynamic than "love of humanity." To love them, we must recall that we who are not worth loving are loved by Love. "For if you love those who love you, what reward will you have? Don't even the tax collectors do the same? And if you greet your brothers only, what great thing are you doing? Don't even the Gentiles do the same? You are to be perfect as your heavenly Father is perfect" (Mt 5:46-48).

A second feature of charity is that it is a habit, not a single act. There is a tremendous amount of sentimental romanticism associated with much human kindness. Remember the great glow you got from giving your overcoat to the beggar on the street, for assisting a blind man up the stairs, for escorting an old woman through traffic, or for contributing a ten dollar bill to relieve an indigent widow. The warmth of self-approval surged through your body, and though you never said it aloud, you did inwardly say: "Gee! I'm Okay!" These good deeds are not to be reproved but commended. But what we wish to emphasize is that nothing has done so much harm to healthy friendliness as the belief that we ought to do one good act a day. Why one good act? What about all the other acts? Charity is a habit, not an isolated act. A husband and wife are out driving. They see a young blonde along the roadside changing a tire. The husband gets out to help her. Would he have done it if the blonde were fifty? He changes the tire, dirties his clothes, cuts his finger, but is all politeness, overflowing sweetness, exuding charm. When he gets back into his own car, his heart aglow with the good deed, his wife says: "I wish you would talk that nice to me. Yesterday when I asked you to bring in the milk you said: 'Are you crippled?'"

See the difference between one act and a habit? Charity is a habit, not a gush or a sentiment; it is a virtue, not an ephemeral thing of moods and impulses; it is a quality of the soul, rather than an individual good deed.

How do you judge a good piano player? By an occasional right note or by the habit or virtue of striking all the right notes? An habitually evil man every now and then may do a good deed. Gangsters endowed soup kitchens and the movies glorified them. But in Christian eyes, this did not prove they were good. Occasionally, an habitually good man may fall, but evil is the *exception* in his life, while it is the *rule* in the life of the gangster. Whether we know it or not, the actions of our daily life are fixing our character for good or for evil. The things you do, the thoughts you think, the words you say, are turning you either into a saint or a devil, to be placed at either the right or the left side of the Divine Judge. If love of God and neighbor becomes a habit of your soul, you are developing heaven within you. But if hatred and evil become the habit of your soul, then you are developing hell within you. Heaven is a place where charity is eternalized. In heaven there will be no faith, for then we will see God; in heaven there will be no hope, for then we will possess God; but in heaven there will be charity, for "love endures forever."

Finally, love is universal. Translating charity's commandment into the concrete, it means that you must love your enemy as you love yourself. Does that mean that you must love Hitler as you love yourself, or the thief who stole your tires, or the woman who said you had so many wrinkles that you had to screw on your hat? It means just that. But how can you love that kind of an enemy as you love yourself?

Well, how do you love yourself? Do you like the way you look? If you did, you would not try to improve it out of a box. Did you ever wish to be anyone else? Why do you lie about your age and say you just turned thirty when you mean you re-turned thirty? Do you like yourself when you develop a sense of rumor, or when you spread gossip and run down your neighbor's reputation, or when you are irritable and moody?

You do not like yourself in these moments. But at the same time, you do love yourself, and you know you do! When you come into a room you invariably pick out the softest chair; you buy yourself good clothes, treat yourself to nice presents; when anyone says you are intelligent or beautiful, you always feel that such a person is of very sound judgment. But when anyone says you are "catty" or selfish, you say they don't understand your good nature, or maybe they are "Fascists."

Thus you love yourself, and yet you do not love yourself. *What* you love about yourself is the person that God made; what you hate about yourself is that God-made person whom you spoiled. You like the sinner, but you hate the sin. That is why, when you do wrong, you ask to be given another chance, or you promise to do better, or you find excuses, or you say, "I was not my true self." But you never deny there is hope.

That is just the way Our Lord intended that you should love your enemies: love them as you love yourself, hating their sin, loving them as sinners; disliking that which blurs the divine image, loving the divine image beneath the blur; never arrogating to yourself a greater right to God's love than they, since deep in your own heart you know that no one could be less deserving of His love than you. And when you see them receiving the just due of their crimes, you do not gloat over them, but say: "There but for the grace of God go I." In this spirit, we are to understand the words of Our Lord: "Love your enemies, do good to those who hate you. Bless those who curse you, and pray for those who insult you. To the one who strikes you on one cheek, offer your other cheek as well. And from the one who takes your cloak, don't hold back your tunic" (Lk 6:27-29). It is Christian to hate the evil of anti-Christians, but not without praying for these enemies that they might be saved — for God loved us when as yet we were sinners.

If, then, you bear a hatred toward anyone, overcome it by doing that person a favor. You can begin to like classical music only by listening to it, and you can make friends out of your enemies only by practicing charity. The reason you love someone else is because that person supplies your lack or fills up your void. You find in the other something you do not have: beauty, wealth, virtue, kindliness, etc.

But God does not love you because you supply His lack. He finds you lovable not because, of and by yourself, you are lovable, but because He puts some of His love in you. As a mother loves her child because her nature is in the child, as the artist loves the canvas because his idea and his colored pattern is in it, so God loves you because His Power or His Nature or His Love is in some way in you.

If, then, God's love for you makes you lovable, why not put some of your love in other people and make them lovable. Where you do not find love, put it there. Love therefore all things, and all persons in God.

> So long as there are poor, I am poor:
> So long as there are prisons, I am a
>   prisoner:
> So long as there are sick, I am weak:
> So long as there is ignorance, I must learn:
> So long as there is hate, I must love.

THE HELL THERE IS

ADDRESS DELIVERED ON FEBRUARY 11, 1945

This is going to be a very unpopular broadcast. It is about a subject the modern mind does not want to hear, namely, hell. Why do our modern minds deny hell? Very simply because they deny sin. If you deny human guilt, then you must deny the right of a state to judge a criminal, or to sentence him to prison. Once you deny the sovereignty of God, you must deny hell. The existence of hell is God's eternal guarantee of the inviolability of human freedom. You can disbelieve in hell, but you must also disbelieve in freedom; you can disbelieve in Sing Sing, but you must also disbelieve in responsibility. You can no more make a free nation without judges and prisons than you can make a free world without Judgment and Hell. No State constitution could exist for six months on the basis of a Liberal Christianity which denies that Christ meant what He said: "Depart from me, you cursed, into the everlasting fire which was prepared for the devil and his angels" (Mt 25:41).

What is the nature of the punishment of hell? It is twofold because it corresponds to the double character of sin. Every mortal sin consists in (a) a turning away from God and (b) a turning to creatures. Because we turn away from God, we feel the absence of His Love, His Beauty, His Truth — and this is called the Pain of Loss. Because we turned to creatures and perverted them to our sinful purpose, we are punished in some way by the very creatures which we abused. This is called the Pain of Sense, one of its aspects being the fire of hell.

The *Pain of Sense* is based on the principle that the punishment should fit the crime. If you disobey one of nature's laws, you suffer a corresponding retribution. If you become intoxicated some night and put yourself in a state of amiable incandescence, you do not necessarily wake up the next morning with an overdrawn bank account. But you do feel the effects of abusing your God-given thirst by something vaguely described as a "hangover." In almost so many words, the alcohol says to you: "I was made by God to be used by you as a reasonable creature. You perverted me from the purpose God intended. Now since I am on God's side, not yours, I shall abuse you, because you abused me." In hell, in like manner, we shall suffer from the very creatures we perverted. Hence there will be different kinds of punishment in hell. The fiercer the grip sinful pleasures had on a soul in this life, the more fiercely will the fires torment it in eternity. As the Scriptures tell us: "Punishment for sin takes the same form as the sin itself" (*Wisdom* 11:16). And do not try to escape this logic or blind yourself to Divine Authority by arguing that hell could not be as you have heard some preachers picture it. I am only saying, do not reject the truth of the book because the pictures are bad.

Now, what is the *Pain of Loss?* That is best understood as the loss of Divine Love, and from three distinct points of view, we shall describe it.

Hell is the hatred of the things you love. A sailor lost on a raft at sea loves water. He was made for it, and water was made for him. He knows that he *ought not* drink the water from the sea, but he violates the dictates of his reason. The result is, he is now more thirsty than before, even thirsty when he is the most filled. He hates water as poison; at the same time he is mad with the thirst for it. In like manner, the soul was made to live on the love of God, but if it perverts that love by salting it with sin, then as the sailor hates the very water he drinks, so the soul hates the very thing it desires, namely, the love of God. As the insane hate most the very persons whom in their saner moments they really love the most, so the damned in hell hate God whom they were really meant to love above all things.

The wicked do not want hell because they enjoy its torments; they want hell because they do not want God. They *need* God, but they do not want Him. Hell is eternal suicide for hating love. Hell is the hatred of the God you love.

Hell is the mind eternally mad at itself for wounding Love. How often during life you have said: "I hate myself." No one who ever condemned you could add to the consciousness of your guilt. You knew it a thousand times better than they. When did you hate yourself most? Certainly not when you failed to act on a tip on the stock market. You hated yourself most when you hurt someone you loved. You even said: "I can never forgive myself for doing that." The souls in hell hate themselves most for wounding Perfect Love. They can *never* forgive themselves. Hence their hell is eternal: eternal self-imposed unforgiveness. It is not that God would not forgive them. It is rather that they will not forgive themselves. How often in this world the sight of moral goodness arouses indignation. The evil person incessantly wants a recasting of all values. Put one good boy in a gang of boys which spends its time in petty thievery or breaking school windows, and the chances are the gang will turn against that good boy, ridicule his moral principles, tell him he is a coward or old-fashioned. Exactly that same mentality is present in adult life. Whenever a professor attacks morality and makes fun of religion before his pupils, you can be sure nine times out of ten that his life is rotten. Goodness is a reproach to such professors: they want everyone to be like themselves, so no one can reproach their conscience. This revolt against goodness and truth is the basic cause of the persecution and mockery of religion today. Now if such things are possible to corrupt souls on earth, why should they not be possible in eternity? These wicked souls will still hate Love because hate is the essence of their souls. They reject the one remedy that could have helped them, the love of Someone besides themselves, and for that reason hell is the house of incurables who hate themselves for hating Love.

Hell is submission to Love under Justice. We are free in this world; we can no more be forced to love God than we can be forced to love classical music, antiques, swing bands, olives, or Bach. Force and love are contraries. Love and freedom are correlatives.

When you came into this world, God said: "I ask you to love me freely, that you may be perfect." Suppose we freely say: "I refuse to love Truth and Justice and Beauty or my neighbor. I shall love error, and graft, and ugliness." Later on you die in that state. But you do not escape that Divine Love which you abused, any more than the traitor escapes the country whose love he despised. Either you possess love, or love possesses you. In marriage a man and woman were meant to possess love. But that love can be perverted so that in the end, love possesses them. How often a husband, for example, tied to a woman by marriage, is possessed by her, by her wants, her selfishness, and her jealousies. Often, too, many a wife is tied to a drunkard or worthless husband until death do them part. They do not freely love one another; they are forced in virtue of the justice of their contracts to love one another until death do them part. And to be forced to love anyone is hell.

The lost souls could have loved God freely. But they chose to rebel against that love, and in doing so came under Divine Justice, as the criminal falls from the love of a country to its justice. The souls in hell do not possess love, love possesses them. Justice forces them to *love* God, that is, to submit to the Divine Order, but to be *forced* to love is the very negation of love. It is hell!

Think not that hell ever ends, or that some day souls in hell will go to heaven. If a soul in hell went to heaven, heaven to it would be a hell. Suppose you hated higher mathematics; suppose your morning paper had nothing in it but logarithms, everyone you met talked to you about Space-Time differentials, every broadcast you heard was on the theory of relativity, every book you read was on the subject of pointer-readings. After a while mathematics would drive you mad. Now the souls in hell hate Perfect Life, Perfect Truth and Perfect Love — which is God — and if they had to live with that which they hated more than you hate mathematics, then God would be their great punishment as mathematics would be yours. Heaven would be hell.

Hell must be eternal. What is the one thing that life can never forgive? Death, because death is the negation of life. What is the one thing that truth can never forgive? Error, for error is its contradiction. What is the one thing that love can never forgive? It is the refusal to love; that is why hell is eternal. Everything does not come out right in the end, for we cannot at one moment believe that we are saved by doing God's will, and the next moment believe that it has no significance. Hell means that the consequences of your good and bad acts are not indifferent. It makes a tremendous amount of difference to your body if you drink tea or TNT, and it makes a greater difference if your soul drinks virtue or vice. Where the tree falls, there it lies.

You ask: "How can a good God be so wrathful as to sentence souls to hell?" Remember that God does not sentence us to hell, as much as we sentence ourselves. When the cage is opened the bird flies out to the air which it loved; when our body dies, the good soul flies out to its eternity of love of God. But a soul in the state of sin at the moment of death casts itself into hell just as naturally as a stone released from my hand falls to the ground.

God has not a different mood for those who go to hell, and for those who go to heaven. The difference is in us, not in Him. The sun which shines on wax softens it; the sun which shines on mud hardens it. There is no difference in the sun, but only in that upon which it shines. So there is no difference in the God of love when He judges the wicked and the just; the difference is in those whom He judges.

Hell is at the foot of the hill of Calvary, and no one of us can go down to hell without first passing over the hill where there is a God-man enthroned with arms outstretched to embrace, head bent to kiss, and heart open to love. I do not find it hard to understand God preparing a hell for those who want to hate themselves eternally for having hated Him. But I do find it hard to understand why that same God should die upon a Cross to save unworthy me from a hell which my sins so rightly deserve. Hell is a place where there is no love. That there may be no hell in our final destinies, one final word: God love you!

THE VALUE OF IGNORANCE

Address Delivered on February 18, 1945

One thousand years before Our Blessed Lord was born, there lived one of the greatest of all poets: the glorious Homer of the Greeks. Two great epics are ascribed to him: one the Iliad, the other the Odyssey. The hero of the Iliad was not Achilles, but Hector, the leader of the enemy Trojans whom Achilles defeated and killed. The poem ends not with a tribute to Achilles, but with a glorification of the defeated Hector. The other poem, the Odyssey, had as its hero, not Odysseus, but Penelope, his wife, who was faithful to him during the years of his travels. As the suitors pressed for her affections, she told them that when she finished weaving the garment they saw before them, she would listen to their courtship. But each night she unraveled what she had woven in the day, and thus remained faithful until her husband returned. "Of all women," she said, "I am the most sorrowful." Well might be applied to her the words of Shakespeare: "Sorrow sits in my soul as on a throne. Bid kings come and bow down to it."

For a thousand years before the birth of Our Blessed Lord, pagan antiquity resounded with these two stories of the poet who threw into the teeth of history the mysterious challenge of glorifying a defeated man and hailing a sorrowful woman. The subsequent centuries asked, how could anyone be victorious in defeat and glorious in sorrow? And the answer was never given until that day when there came One who was glorious in defeat: the Christ on His Cross; and one who was magnificent in sorrow: His Blessed Mother beneath the Cross.

It is interesting that Our Lord spoke seven times on Calvary and that His Mother is recorded as having spoken seven times in Sacred Scripture. Her last recorded word was at the Marriage Feast of Cana, when her Divine Son began His public life. Now that the sun was out, there was no longer need of the moon to shine. Now that the Word had spoken, there was no longer need of words.

One wonders, as Our Blessed Lord spoke each of His Seven Words, if Our Blessed Mother at the foot of the Cross did not think of each of her corresponding Words? Such will be the subject of our Lenten meditations: Our Lord's Seven Words on the Cross and the Seven Words of Mary's life.

Generally, when innocent men suffer at the hands of impious judges, their last words are either,

"I am innocent" or "The courts are rotten." But here for the first time in the hearing of the world is one who asked neither for the forgiveness of His own sins, for He is God, nor proclaimed His own innocence, for men are not judges of God. Rather does He plead for those who kill Him: "Father, forgive them, for they know not what they do" (Lk 28:34).

Mary, beneath the Cross, heard her Divine Son speak that First Word. I wonder, when she heard Him say "know not," if she did not recall her own First Word. It too, contained those words, "know not." The occasion was the Annunciation, the first good news to reach the earth in centuries. The angel announced to her that she was to become the Mother of God: "'Behold, you will conceive in your womb, and will bear a son; and you shall name him Jesus…'; and Mary said to the angel: 'How will this come about, since I know not man?'" (Lk 1:31-34).

These words of Jesus and Mary seem to suggest that there is sometimes wisdom in not knowing. Ignorance is here represented not as a curse, but as a blessing. This rather shocks our modern sensibilities concerning education — but that is because we fail to distinguish between true wisdom and false wisdom. St. Paul called the wisdom of the world "foolishness with God" (1 Cor 1:20), and Our Blessed Lord thanked His Heavenly Father that He had not revealed Heavenly Wisdom to the worldly wise (Mt 11:25).

The ignorance which is here extolled is not ignorance of the truth, but ignorance of evil. Notice it first of all in the word of Our Savior to His executioners: He implied that they could be forgiven only because they were ignorant of their terrible crime. It was not their wisdom that would save them, but their ignorance. In like manner if we knew what we were doing when we smote the Hands of Everlasting Mercy, dug the Feet of the Good Shepherd, crowned the Head of Wisdom Incarnate, and still went on doing it, we would never be saved. We would be damned! It is only our ignorance which brings us within the pale of redemption and forgiveness. As St. Peter told them on Pentecost: "I know that you did it through ignorance, as did also your rulers" (Ac 3:17).

The First Word our Blessed Mother spoke at the Annunciation revealed the same lesson. She said: "I know not man." Why was there a value in not knowing man? Because she had consecrated her virginity to God. At a moment when every woman sought the privilege of being the Mother of the Messiah, Mary gave up the hope — and received the privilege. She refuses to discuss with an angel any kind of compromise with her high resolve. If the condition of becoming the Mother of God was the surrender of her vow, she would not make that surrender, knowing man would have been evil for her — though it would not have been evil in other circumstances. Not knowing man is a kind of ignorance, but here it proves to be such a blessing that in an instant the Holy Spirit overshadows her, making her a living ciborium privileged to bear within herself for nine months the Guest who is the Host of the world.

You live in a world in which the worldly wise say: "You do not know life; you have never lived." They assume that you can know nothing except by experience — experience not only of good but of evil.

Examine your own life. If you know evil by experience, are you wiser because of it? Do you not now despise that very evil, and are you not the more tragic for having experienced it? You may even have become mastered by the evil you experienced. How often the disillusioned say: "I wish I had never tasted liquor," or "I regret the day I stole my first dollar," or "I wish I had never known that person." How much wiser you would have been had you been ignorant!

Think not, then, that in order to "know life" you must "experience evil." Is a doctor wiser because he is prostrate with disease? Do we know cleanliness by living in sewers? Do you become a better pianist by striking the wrong keys?

Do not excuse yourself by saying "temptations

are too strong," or "good people do not know what temptation is." The good know more about the strength of temptations than those who fall. How do you know how strong the enemy is in battle? By being captured or by conquering? How can you know the strength of a temptation unless you overcome it? Our Blessed Lord really understands the power of temptation better than anyone, because He overcame the temptations of Satan.

There is so much evil in the world today, so many lies propagated, so many ideas known that are untrue, that it would be a great blessing if some generous soul would endow a University for unlearning. Its purpose would be to do with error and evil exactly what doctors do with disease! Well, such an institution does exist and here are two practical courses it offers for unlearning evil.

1. If you are a Catholic, go to confession and have your sins blotted out, for here is an act as great as creation. In making the world, God made something out of nothing; in forgiving, God put something into nothing, namely your sins. Would you not like to be right now just as you were when you came from the hands of God at the baptismal font, with no false wisdom yet gathered to your mind so that, like an empty chalice, you might spend your life filling it with the wisdom of His Love? Honestly, if you had the choice now either of learning more about the world or of unlearning the evil you know,

would you not rather unlearn than learn? Well, that is what absolution does; it makes you wise by ignorance. You will not be given a sheepskin when you walk out of the confessional box, that great University of Unlearning, but you will feel like a lamb, for Christ will be your Shepherd.

2. A second way to unlearn evil is to spend a Holy Hour a day in meditation. This can be done by everyone, whether you be Jew, Protestant, or Catholic. If you are a Catholic, spend that hour in the presence of Our Lord in the Blessed Sacrament, making your morning Mass the first half of that hour. Be ignorant of propaganda, politics, economics, and gossip for an hour a day and become truly wise being instructed by the Spirit of God. You need to get away from the world now and then to know what you ought to be. God writes better on a blank page than on one covered with your scribblings.

People living in dirt hardly ever realize how dirty dirt is. Those who live in sin hardly understand the horror of sin. The one peculiar and terrifying thing about sin is, the more experience you have with it, the less you know about it. You become so identified with it that you know neither the depths to which you have sunk, nor the heights from which you have fallen. You never know you were asleep until you wake up; and you never know the horror of sin until you get out of sin. Hence, only the sinless really know what sin is. One hour a day spent with God in meditation will help you unlearn your sin. Since there on the Cross and in its shadow there is Innocence at its highest, it follows that there was also the greatest sorrow. Since there was no sin, there was the greatest understanding of its evil. It was their innocence which made the agonies of Calvary so tragic.

St. Thomas Aquinas tells us that the least love of God is worth more than the knowledge of all created things, because by knowing the world we identify ourselves with the corruptible, but by loving God we become assimilated to Eternal Perfection.

We all *know* enough to be better than we are; our unhappiness comes from our want of love.

THE SECRET OF SANCTITY

ADDRESS DELIVERED ON FEBRUARY 25, 1945

There is one thing in the world that is definitely and absolutely your own, and that is your will. Health, power, life, and honor can all be snatched from you, but your will is irrevocably your own, even in hell. Hence, nothing really matters in life, except what you do with your will. It is the drama of will which makes the story of the two thieves crucified on either side of Our Lord one of the absorbing incidents of history.

Both thieves at first blasphemed. There was no such thing as the good thief at the beginning of the Crucifixion. But when the thief on the right heard that Man on the Central Cross forgive His executioners, he had a change of soul. He began to accept his sorrows. He took up his cross as a yoke rather than as a gibbet, abandoned himself to God's will, and turning to the rebellious thief on the left said: "Have you no fear of God, seeing that you are under the same condemnation! And we indeed justly, for the sentence we received corresponds to our crimes: but this man has done nothing wrong." Then from his heart already so full of surrender to his Savior, there came this plea, "Remember me when you come into your kingdom." Immediately there came the answer of the Lord, "Amen, I say to you, this day you shall be with me in Paradise" (Lk 23:40-43).

"You." We are all individuals in the sight of God. He calls His sheep by name. This Word was the foundation of Christian democracy. Every soul is precious in God's sight, even those whom the State casts out and kills. At the foot of the Cross, Mary witnessed the conversion of the good thief, and her soul rejoiced that he had accepted the will of God. Her Divine Son's Second Word promising Paradise as a reward for that surrender, reminded her of her own Second Word some thirty years before, when the angel had appeared to her and told her that she was to be the Mother of Him who was now dying on the Cross. In her First Word she asked how this would be accomplished since she knew not man. But when the angel said she would conceive of the Holy Spirit, Mary immediately answered: "Be it done to me according to your word." *Fiat mihi secundum verbum tuum* (Lk 1:38).

This was one of the great Fiats of the world. The first was at Creation when God said: *Fiat lux:* "Let there be light." Another was in Gethsemane when the Savior, pressing the chalice of redemption to His lips, cried: *Fiat voluntas tua:* "Your will be done" (Mt 26:42). The third was Mary's, pronounced in a Nazarene cottage, which proved to be a declaration of war against the empire of evil: *Fiat mihi secundum verbum tuum.* "Be it done to me according to your word" (Lk 1:38).

The Second Word of Jesus on Golgotha and the Second Word of Mary in Nazareth teach the same lesson: *Everyone in the world has a cross, but the cross is not the same for any two of us.* The cross of the thief was not the cross of Mary. The difference was due to God's will toward each. The thief was to give his life; Mary to accept life. The thief was to hang on his cross; Mary to remain behind. The thief received a dismissal; Mary received a mission. The thief was to be received into Paradise; but Paradise was to be received into Mary.

Each of us, too, has a cross. Our Lord said: "If anyone would be my disciple, he must deny himself, and take up his cross, and follow me" (Mk 8:34). He did not say: "Take up My Cross." His cross is not the same as yours, and yours is not the same as mine. Every cross in the world is tailor made, custom built, patterned to fit its bearer and no one else.

That is why we say: "My cross is heavy." We assume that other people's crosses are lighter, forgetful that the only reason our cross is heavy is simply because it is our own. Our Lord did not make His cross; It was made for Him. So yours is made by the circumstances of your life, and by your routine duties. That is why it fits so tight. Crosses are not made by machines.

Our Lord deals separately with each of our souls. The crown of gold you want may have underneath it the crown of thorns, but the heroes who choose the crown of thorns, often find that underneath it is the crown of gold. Even those that seem to be without a cross actually have one. No one would have suspected that when Mary resigned herself to God's will by accepting the honor of becoming the Mother of God she would ever have to bear a cross. It would seem, too, that one who was preserved free from original sin should be dispensed from the penalties of that sin, such as pain. And yet this honor brought to her seven crosses and ended by making her the Queen of Martyrs.

There are, therefore, as many kinds of crosses as there are persons: crosses of grief and sorrow, crosses of want, crosses of abuse, crosses of wounded love, and crosses of defeat!

There is the cross of widows. How often Our Lord spoke of them; for example, in the parable of the judge and the widow (Lk 18:1-8); when He rebuked the Pharisees who "devoured widows' houses" (Mk 12:40); when He spoke to the widow of Nain (Lk 7:12); and when He praised the widow who threw two mites into the temple treasury (Mk 12:42). Widowhood may have been particularly dear to Him because His own mother was a widow, for Joseph His foster father was presumably already dead.

There is the cross of death when God takes someone from you, as He may be doing in this war. It is always for a good reason. When the sheep have grazed and thinned the grass in the lower regions, the shepherd will take a little lamb in his arms, carry it up the mountain where the grass is green, lay it down, and soon the other sheep will follow. Every now and then Our Blessed Lord, too, takes a lamb from the parched pasture of a family up to those Heavenly Green Pastures, that the rest of the family may keep their eyes on their true home and follow through.

Then there is the cross of sickness, which always has a divine purpose. Our Blessed Lord said of a particular illness: "This sickness will not bring death — it is for the glory of God" (Jn 11:4). Resignation to this particular kind of cross is one of the very highest forms of prayer. Unfortunately, the sick generally want to be doing something else than being sick which God has willed at least permissively. The tragedy of this world is not so much the pain in it; the tragedy is that so much of that pain is wasted.

It is only when a log is thrown into the fire that it begins to sing. It was only when the thief was thrown into the fire of a cross that he found God. It is only in pain that some discover Love.

Because our crosses differ, soul will differ from soul in glory. We think too often that in heaven there is going to be somewhat the same inequality in social positions that we have here; that servants on earth will be servants in heaven; that the important people on earth will be the important people in heaven. This is not true. God will take into account our crosses. He seemed to suggest that in the parable of Dives and Lazarus: "My child, remember that you received what was good in your lifetime, while Lazarus likewise received what was bad; but now he is comforted here, whereas you are tormented" (Lk 16:25). There will be a bright jewel of merit for those who suffer in this world. Because we live in a world where position is determined economically, we forget that in God's world the royalty are those who do His will. Heaven will be a complete reversal of the values of earth. The first shall be last and the last first, for God is no respecter of persons. A wealthy and socially important woman went to heaven. St. Peter pointed to a beautiful mansion and said, "This is your chauffeur's home." "Well," said she, "if that is his home, think what mine will be like." Pointing to a tiny cottage, Peter said, "There is yours." "I can't live in that," she answered. And Peter said, "I'm sorry, that is the best I could do with the material you sent up to me." Those who suffer as the good thief did, have sent ahead some fine material.

It makes no difference, then, what you do here on earth; what matters is the love with which you do it. The street cleaner who accepts in God's name a cross arising from his state in life, such as the scorn of his fellow men; the mother who pronounces her *Fiat* to the Divine Will as she raises a family for the Kingdom of God; the afflicted in hospitals who say *Fiat* to their cross of suffering, are the uncanonized saints; for what is sanctity but fixation in goodness by abandonment to God's Holy Will?

It is typically American to feel that we are not doing anything unless we are doing something *big*. But from the Christian point of view, there is no one thing that is bigger than any other thing. The bigness comes from the way our wills utilize things. Hence mopping an office for the love of God is "bigger" than running the office for the love of money.

Each of us is to praise and love God in his own way. The bird praises God by singing, the flower by blooming, the clouds with their rain, the sun with its light, the moon with its reflection, and each of us by our patient resignation to the trials of our state in life.

If the gold in the bowels of the earth did not say *Fiat* to the miner and the goldsmith, it would never become the chalice on the altar; if the pencil did not say *Fiat* to the hand of the writer, we would never have the poem; if Our Lady did not say *Fiat* to the angel, she would never have become the House of God; if Our Lord did not say *Fiat* to the Father's will in Gethsemane, we would never have been redeemed; if the thief did not say *Fiat* in his heart, he never would have been the escort for the Master into Paradise.

The reason most of us are what we are, mediocre Christians, "up" one day, "down" the next, is simply because we refuse to let God work on us. As crude marble, we rebel against the hand of the sculptor; as unvarnished canvas, we shrink from the oils and tints of the Heavenly Artist. We are so "fearful lest having Him we may have naught else beside," forgetful that if we have the fire of Love, why worry about the sparks, and if we have the perfect round, why trouble ourselves with the arc. We always make the fatal mistake of thinking that it is what we do that matters, when really what matters is what we let God do to us. God sent the angel to Mary, not to ask her to do something, but to let something be done.

Since God is a better artisan than you, the more you abandon yourself to Him, the happier He can make you. It is well to be a self-made man, but it is better to be a God-made man. Try it — I mean you, whether you be Jew, Protestant, or Catholic — by spending a Holy Hour a day in prayer and meditation. Catholics should include morning Mass in their Hour, thus taking advantage of Calvary's sacrifice, in a world of lesser Calvaries.

God will love you, of course, even though you do not love Him; but remember, if you give Him only half your heart, He can make you only 50% happy.

You have freedom only to give it away. To whom do you give yours? You give it either to the moods, the hour, to your egotism, to creatures, or to God.

Do you know that, if you give your freedom to God, in heaven you will have no freedom of choice, because once you possess the Perfect, there is nothing left to choose; and still you will be perfectly free, because you will be one with Him whose heart is Freedom and Love.

THE FELLOWSHIP OF RELIGION

ADDRESS DELIVERED ON MARCH 4, 1945

This war has proved that human beings are morally closer to one another in a bomb shelter or foxhole than they are in a brokerage office or at a bridge table. Sorrow draws hearts together. Given therefore the tragedy of Calvary, one should expect to find Our Lord and His Blessed Mother and all humanity in the deepest fellowship of religion.

St. John prefaces the Word Our Lord spoke to His Mother from the Cross by the mention of the Lord's seamless garment for which the soldiers were now shaking dice.

Why, out of all the details of the Passion, should he suddenly begin thinking about a robe? Because it was woven by Mary's hands. It was such a beautiful robe that these hardened criminals refused to tear it apart. Custom gave them the right to the perquisites of those whom they crucified. But here the criminals refused to divide the spoils. They shook dice for it, so that the winner could have the whole robe.

After having yielded up His garment to those who gambled for it, He on the Cross now yields up her who wove it. Our Blessed Lord looks down to the two most beloved creatures He has on earth: Mary and John. He speaks first to His Blessed Mother. He does not call her "Mother," but "Woman." As St. Bernard so lovingly suggests, if He had called her "Mother," she would have been just His Mother and no one else's. In order to indicate that she is now becoming the Mother of all men whom He redeems, He endows her with the title of universal motherhood: "Woman." Then indicating with a gesture of His head the presence of His beloved disciple, He added: "Behold your son." He does not call him John, for if He did, John would have been only the son of Zebedee; He left him unnamed that he might stand for all humanity.

Our Lord was equivalently saying to His Mother: "You already have one Son, and I am He. You cannot have another. All the other sons will be in Me as the branches are in the vine. Hence I say not, 'Behold another son!' but 'Behold your son.'"

As she was the custodian of the Vine so now she would be custodian of the branches through time and eternity. In Bethlehem she had given birth to the King; now on Calvary she was begetting the Kingdom. At the crib Mary was the Madonna of the Son of God. At the cross Mary became our Madonna.

When Mary heard Our Blessed Lord speak

His Third Word establishing this new relationship, she remembered so very well when it began. Her Third Word, as His, was about relationship. It was a long time ago. After the angel announced to her that she was to be the Mother of God, which alone would have bound her to all humanity, the angel added that her elderly cousin, Elizabeth, was now six months with child. "In those days Mary set out and went with solicitude into the hill country to a city of Juda. And when she entered the house of Zachary, she greeted Elizabeth" (Lk 1:39-40).

It is rightly assumed that no one may more justly claim immunity from service to others than a woman bearing a child. If one adds to this, *noblesse oblige,* the fact that this Woman bears within herself the very Lord of the Universe, then of all creatures Mary might rightfully claim dispensation from social bonds and duties to neighbor. Women in that condition are not to minister but to be ministered to. But here we have the spectacle of the greatest of all women becoming the servant of others. Not standing on her dignity saying, "I am the Mother of God," but recognizing the need of her aged cousin, the pregnant Queen, instead of awaiting her hour in isolation like other women, mounts a donkey, makes a five day journey over hill country, and with such a consciousness of spiritual fellowship that she does it, in the language of Sacred Scripture, "with solicitude."

Before the Savior is born, Mary recognizes that her mission is to bring the Savior to humanity; and with such a holy impatience is she filled, that she begins it before her Son has seen the light of day. I love to think of her on this journey as the first Christian Nurse whose service to neighbor is inseparable from bringing Christ into the life of her patient.

There is no record of the exact words that Mary spoke. The Evangelist merely tells us that she greeted Elizabeth. But notice that just as soon as she greeted her cousin, new relationships were immediately established. Elizabeth no longer addressed her as cousin. She calls her: "The mother of my Lord" (Lk 1:43). But that was not the end of the relationship. Elizabeth's own child — who was to be called later by Our Lord, "The greatest man ever born of woman" — now stirs in his mother's womb. As Elizabeth said: "For, behold, when the sound of your greeting came to my ears, the baby in my womb leapt for joy" (Lk 1:44). We might almost say John the Baptist danced to his birth in salutation to the King of Kings! Two unborn children establish a relationship before either had swung open the portals of flesh.

Every record we have of our Blessed Lady is one of bringing Christ into humanity. First of all, it was through her as a Gate of Heaven that He walked into this earth. It was in her as a Mirror of Justice that He first saw with human eyes the reflection of the world He had made. It is in her as a kind of living ciborium that He is carried to the First Communion rail of her cousin's home, where an unborn babe salutes Him as the Host who is to be the Guest of the world. It is through her intercession at Cana that He brings His Divine Power to supply a human need. And it is finally at the Cross that she who gave Christ to the world, now receives Him back again in us who have the high and undeserved honor to call ourselves Christians.

Because of this Divinely established intimacy I wonder if it is not true that as the world loses veneration for Christ's Mother, it loses also its adoration of Christ. Is it not true in earthly relationships that, as a so-called friend ignores your mother when he comes to your home, sooner or later he will ignore you as well? Conversely, as the world begins knocking at Mary's door, it will find that Our Lord Himself will answer.

How shall we escape this conclusion? If Christ Himself willed to be physically formed in her for nine months and then be spiritually formed by her for thirty years, is it not to her that we must go to learn how to have Christ formed in us? Only she who raised Christ can raise a Christian.

That is why every single broadcast I give is dedicated to Our Lady, in the hope that as the sponsor of each broadcast she may bring her Divine Son into your souls as she brought Him to Elizabeth, John, and to the young married couple at Cana.

So firmly convinced am I that it is through Mary that the world will find Our Lord again, that I am going to ask every one of you of good will to say the Rosary daily for this intention.

What favors may you expect from a daily recitation of the Rosary?

1. You will never lose your soul if you say it daily and cooperate with God's grace.

2. Your family will be blessed in peace and war if you say the Rosary every night in the family circle.

3. If you desire to bring a soul to the fullness of God's faith and charity, teach that person to say the Rosary. He will either stop saying the Rosary or will receive the gift of Faith.

Finally, the purpose of the Rosary is to bring you to God. Mary is treacherous in the sense that she will betray you into the hands of her Divine Son.

As Francis Thompson bade her:

The celestial Temptress play,
And all mankind to bliss betray;
With sacrosanct cajoleries
And starry treachery of your eyes,
Tempt us back to Paradise!

Since Our Lord gave His Mother to us on the Cross, then we are her children, and as such we say to her in the language of Mary Dixon Thayer:

Lovely Lady dressed in blue
Teach me how to pray!
God was just your little Boy,
Tell me what to say!
Did you lift Him up, sometimes,
Gently, on your knee?
Did you sing to Him the way
Mother does to me?
Did you hold his hand at night?
Did you ever try
Telling stories of the world
O! And did He cry?
Do you really think He cares
If I tell Him things —
Little things that happen? And
Do the Angels' wings
Make a noise? And can He hear
Me if I speak low?
Tell me — for you know.
Lovely Lady dressed in blue
Teach me how to pray!
God was just your little Boy
And you know the way.*

---

* The poem *To Our Lady* by Mary Dixon Thayer quoted with the permission of the Macmillan Company.

CONFIDENCE IN VICTORY

Perhaps at no time in modern history was there ever such a flight from life as at the present day.

Also, there is the flight from consciousness through alcoholism, or the flight from decision through religious indifference, or the flight from freedom by the denial of responsibility. All these are symptoms of despair. Many people as a result are cracking up, emotionally, mentally, and morally. But our problem is not to diagnose the malady, but to heal it.

Is there another way out, even in these dark days? For an answer one must go back to the darkest day the world ever saw, the day when the sun hid its face at noon, as if ashamed to shed its light on the crime men committed at Calvary. As darkness spread over the earth three crosses became silhouetted against a black horizon. We see nothing; there is only an awful silence, a thick gloom, relieved by one cry, sent up from a broken heart of self-abasement: "My God, My God, why have you forsaken me?" (Mk 15:34).

These words were the first words of prophetic Psalm 21, written about a thousand years before this black day. Though the Psalm begins with this cry of sadness, if Our Lord had finished reciting it He would have ended with words of joy, victory, and the promise to feed the hungry and to establish spiritual sovereignty over the earth.

Mary, standing at the foot of the Cross, knew her scriptures well. When she heard Our Lord begin Psalm 21 it reminded her of a song that she once sang. It was her Fourth Word which she chanted in the home of Elizabeth, the greatest song ever written — *The Magnificat*: "My soul magnifies the Lord." The end of her song contains very much the same sentiments as the end of Psalm 21, namely, that her Divine Son would feed the poor, exalt her among nations, and that His victory would endure forever.

There is something common to both these songs: both were spoken before there was any assurance of victory. In His Fourth Word from the Cross, the suffering figure looks forward through the darkness to the triumph of the Resurrection and His spiritual dominion over the earth. In her Fourth Word the woman, nine months before her child is born, looks down the long procession of the coming ages, and proclaims that when the world's great women like Livia, Julia, and Octavia shall have been forgotten, the ordinary law of human oblivion will be suspended in her favor, because she is the Mother of Him whose Name is Holy, and who would make her remembered from generation to generation because His Cross is the redemption of men.

Both were really words of triumph, one of victory before the battle was over, one of Overlordship before the Lord was born. To both Jesus and Mary, there were treasures in darkness, whether the darkness be on a black hill or in a dark womb.

Are you in the valley of despair? Then learn that the Gospel of Christ can be heard as Good News even by those whose life has been shattered by Bad News, for only those who walk in darkness ever see the stars. The reason therefore why some souls emerge purified from catastrophe, while other souls come out worse, is because the first had One in whom they could trust and the second had none but themselves. The atheist, therefore, is properly defined as the person who has no invisible means of support.

Have you ever noticed, as you talked to your fellow men, the different reactions of those who have faith in God and His purposes, and those who have not? The man without faith was generally greatly surprised at the dark turn of events with two world wars in 21 years, with the resurgence of barbarism, and the abandonment of moral principles. But the man with faith in God was not so surprised. The sum came out just as he had expected; chaos was in the cards, though they had not yet been dealt, for he knew that "Unless the Lord build the house, they labor in vain who build it" (Ps 126:1).

H.G. Wells, for example, whose optimism once hoped that "man with his feet on earth, would one day have hands reaching among the stars," became pessimistic as darkness fell over the earth in these last few years. Now he says that "the universe is bored with man, is turning a hard face to him; and I see him being carried more and more rapidly... along the stream of fate to degradation, suffering and death."

Now hear St. Paul, a man of faith who lived in dark days too. He had been persecuted and he knew that the tyrant who held the sword would one day draw it across his neck, yet in full trust he says: "Who then shall separate us from the love of Christ? Shall tribulation? or distress? or famine? or nakedness, or danger? or persecution? or the sword? ...For I am sure that neither death, nor life, nor angels, nor principalities, nor powers, nor things present, nor things to come, nor might, nor height, nor depth, nor any other creature shall be able to separate us from the love of God, which is in Christ Jesus Our Lord" (Rm 8:35, 38-39).

You see the difference? Now choose! Will you

slip down into abysmal despair, or will you, like Christ in a blackness at high noon, and like Mary before her Tree of Life had seen the earth, trust in God, His mercy, and His victory?

If you are unhappy, or sad, or despondent, it is basically for only one reason: you have refused to respond to Love's plea: "Come to me, all you who labor and are heavy burdened, and I will give you rest" (Mt 11:29). Everywhere else but in Him, the liberation promised is either armed or forced, and that can mean slavery. Only *nailed* love is free. Unnailed and crucified love can compel. But hands pinioned to a wooden beam cannot force, nor can a lifted Host and an elevated Chalice constrain — but they can beckon and solicit.

That kind of love gives you these three suggestions for living in troubled times:

1. Never forget that there are only two philosophies to rule your life: The one of the Cross which starts with the fast and ends with the feast; the other of Satan, which starts with the feast and ends with the headache. Unless there is the Cross, there will never be the empty tomb; unless there is faith in darkness, there will never be vision in light; unless there is a Good Friday there will never be an Easter Sunday.

2. When bereavement comes, when the "slings and arrows of outrageous fortune" strike, when like Simon of Cyrene a cross is laid on your reluctant

shoulders, then I say to you who are Catholics, take that cross to daily Mass, as part of your daily Holy Hour and say to Our Lord at the moment of consecration: "As You my Savior in love for me say: 'This is My Body! This is My Blood!' so I say to You: 'This is my body! Take it. This is my blood! Take it. They are yours. I care not if the accidents or "species" of my life remain, such as my daily work, my routine duties, but all that I am substantially, take, consecrate, ennoble, spiritualize so that I am no longer mine, but Yours, O Lord Divine.'"

3. In your daily Holy Hour of prayers and meditation, whether you be Jew, Protestant or Catholic, think not of Almighty God as a kind of absentee landlord with whom you hardly dare to be familiar. Do not fear Him with a servile fear, for God is more patient with you than you are with yourself. Would you, for example, be as patient with the wicked world today as He is? Would you even be as patient with anyone else who had the same faults as you? Rather approach Him in full confidence and even with the boldness of a loving child who has a right to ask a Father for favors.

Though He may not grant all you desire, be sure that in a certain sense there is no unanswered prayer. A child asks his father for something that may not be good for him — for example, a gun. The father, while refusing, will pick up the child in his arms to console him, giving the response of love, even in the denial of a request. As the child forgets in that embrace that he ever asked a favor, so in praying you forget what you wanted when you receive what you really need: communion with Divine Love. Do not forget either, that there are not two kinds of answers to prayer, but three: One is "Yes." Another is "No." The third is "Wait."

You will find that, as you pray, the nature of your requests will change. You will ask less and less things for yourself, and more and more for His love. Is it not true in human relationships that the more you love someone, the more you seek to give and the less you desire to receive. The deepest love never says, "Give me," but it does say, "Take." You probably think that if Our Lord came into your room some night as you were praying, you would ask Him favors, or present your difficulties, or say: "When will the war end?" or "Should I buy General Motors stock?" or "Give me a million dollars."

No! You would throw yourself on your knees and kiss the hem of His garment. And the moment He laid His hands on your head you would feel such a peace and trust and confidence — even in the darkness — that you would not even remember you had questions to ask, or favors to beg. You would consider them a kind of desecration. You would want only to look into His face, and you would be in a world which only lovers know. That would be the Heaven you wanted!

RELIGION IS A QUEST

Address Delivered on March 18, 1945

Every human heart in the world without exception is on the quest of God. Not everyone may be conscious of it, but it is as natural for the soul to want God as for the body to want food or drink. It was natural for the prodigal son to be hungry; it was unnatural to live on husks. It is natural to want God; it is unnatural to satisfy that want with false gods.

Not only is the soul on the quest of God, but God is on the quest of the soul, not because He needs us, but because we need Him.

This double quest of the Creator for the creature and the creature for the Creator is revealed in the Fifth Word of Our Lord from the Cross, and the Fifth Word of Our Lady, pronounced when her Son was only twelve years of age.

One day Our Blessed Lord said to the multitude: "If anyone thirst, let him come to me and drink" (Jn 7:87). But on the Cross, He from whose fingertips toppled planets and worlds, He who filled the valleys with the song of a thousand fountains, now cries not to God but to man: "I thirst" (Jn 19:28). And yet that thirst could not have been only physical, for the Gospel tells us that He spoke in order that the Scriptures might be fulfilled. It therefore was spiritual as well as physical. God was on the quest of souls, trusting that one of the trivial ministrations of life, the offering of a cup in His name, might bring the offerer within the sweet radiance of His grace.

Mary, standing in the shadow of her Son's hard deathbed, heard His Word and was reminded of the time she thirsted, too. It was when her little Son, who had reached the age of twelve, was lost during the pilgrimage she and Joseph made to the Holy City. If the trumpets of doom had sounded, their hearts would have been less heavy. For three days they flushed the hills and caravans, and on the third day they found Him. We know not where He was during those three days. We can only guess. Perhaps He was visiting Gethsemane where His blood twenty-one years later would crimson the olive roots; perhaps He stood on Calvary's hill and looked forward to this sad hour. In any case, on the third day they found Him in the Temple, teaching the doctors of the law. Mary said: "Son, why have you done this to us? Your father and I have been worried to death looking for you" (Lk 2:48). In a land where women were reticent, where men were masters, it was not Joseph who spoke; it was Mary. Mary was the virgin mother, Joseph was the foster father.

Here was a creature on the quest of God. As our Blessed Lord's thirst on the Cross revealed the Creator in search of man, Mary's words revealed its complementary truth, that the creature is in search of God.

If each is seeking for the other, why do they not find? God does not always find man because man is free, and like Adam he can hide from God. Like a child who hides from his mother when he does something wrong, so does man turn from God when he sins. God then always seems "so far away"; but the truth is, it is man who is "far away." Sin creates a distance. Respecting human freedom, God calls but He does not force. "I thirst" is the language of liberty. Man in his turn does not always find God because he gives up his search too quickly. God is found on the third day, for in the language of Our Lord, that is the day of perfection.

God is closer to us than we know:

> "The angels keep their ancient places;
> Turn but a stone, and start a wing!
> 'Tis ye, 'tis your estranged faces,
> That miss the many-splendored thing."*

---

* From *Kingdom of God*, by Francis Thompson.

If, then, you are interested in saving souls, always start with the assumption that everyone wants God, and God loves everyone.

How about bigots? Do they want Our Lord and His Church? Certainly! Sometimes their hatred is a vain attempt to ignore. Never be too hard on bigots. They do not really hate the Church. They hate only what they mistakenly believe to be the Church. If I had heard the same lies about the Church they have heard, and if I had been taught the same historical perversions, with my own peculiar character and temperament I would hate the Church ten times more than they do. At least they have some zeal and some fire. It may be misdirected, but with God's grace it can be channeled into love. These souls who peddle anti-religious tracts or anti-Catholic publications are to be regarded in exactly the same light as St. Paul before his conversion. And as he preached and lectured against the Church, after assisting at the killing of the most brilliant of the early churchmen, St. Stephen, there were many believers who despaired. Prayers were multiplied to God: "Send someone to refute Paul." And God heard their prayers. God sent Paul to answer Paul. A bigot made the best Apostle.

In my radio audience a few years ago was a young woman who used to sit before the radio and ridicule and scoff at every word. She is now enjoying the fullness of Faith and the Sacraments. In another town was a man who used to make records of these broadcasts, then take them to a nearby convent and play them for the sisters who had no radio. But he mitigated this act of kindness by making a running commentary of ridicule while the record played. He recently built the Sisters a new school in that city. Everyone is on the quest of God, and if the soul gives God a chance, God will win.

How about those who lost the faith? Here I refer in particular to the fallen-away Catholic. His fall is serious because of the height from which he fell. Is God thirsting for him? Obviously, for the Good Shepherd never gives up seeking His lost sheep.

On the other hand, the fallen-away, too, thirsts for reunion with Our Lord and His Body, the Church, but in an oblique sort of way. Having tasted the best, he is miserable without it; having eaten the Bread of Life all else makes hungry where most it satisfies. Because wandering sheep are brokenhearted without the Shepherd, make it a rule never to argue with a fallen-away Catholic. If, for example, any such tells you that he no longer believes in confession, do not believe it. Like the woman at the well, who had five husbands, he wants to keep religion in the realm of speculation. What he needs is to have it brought down to the realm of the moral, as Our Blessed Lord did for that woman. He wants an argument to salve his conscience, but he needs absolution to heal it.

If there be any such soul in my audience, please go to confession during Holy Week and recover the peace which only God can give. If there is anything I can do to help your return, please call on me, for I assure you the greatest joy of a priest's heart comes from lifting sheep from the thorns and brambles into the embrace of the Shepherd of Life.

Do sinners want God too? Conscious sinners do. That is why one need hardly ever tell such a sinner how wicked he is. He knows it a thousand times better than you. His conscience has pointed an accusing finger at him in his sleep; his fears have emblazoned his sins on his mind; his neuroses, anxieties, and unhappiness have been like trumpets of his inner death. The Divine Savior wants sinners particularly, for He said that He came to save not the just but the sinners.

His pardoning grace will save you, if you do not lock it out. In that case you would be like the cobbler mentioned by Charles Dickens. For years he had been a prisoner in the Bastille, where he cobbled shoes. He became so enamored of the walls, the darkness, and the monotony of his task, that when he was liberated he built a cell at the center of his English home, and on days when skies were clear and birds were singing, the taps of the cobbler in the dark could still be heard. So men by habitual residence in imprisoning moods render themselves incapable of living in the wider horizons of God's grace.

Do I hear you object: "But I am a sinner. God will not hear me." If God will not hear a sinner, why did He praise the publican in the rear of the temple, who struck his breast saying: "O God, be merciful to me a sinner" (Lk 18:13)? There were two sinners on Calvary on either side of Our Lord. One was saved because he asked to be saved. Did not Our Divine Savior say: "Come to me, all you who labor and are heavy burdened" (Mt 12:28)? And who is more heavily burdened than a sinner?

Do not stunt your spiritual life by looking always for your faults. Think of God's love. Never despair! Not until God ceases to be infinitely good and you begin to be infinitely wicked have you a right to be hopeless.

If you still insist that you never before prayed in your life and therefore God would not listen to you now, my answer is: Pray anyway. A strange voice is always the one most quickly heard.

THE PURPOSE OF LIFE

Address Delivered on March 25, 1945

There is no word more often used in our modern world and more often misunderstood than the word *freedom*. Almost everyone thinks of it as freedom *from* something, but rarely as freedom *for* something. Some think they are free only because they have no ball and chain on their feet, without ever adverting to why they want to be free, and what is the purpose of life.

The root of all our trouble is that freedom for God and in God has been interpreted as freedom from God. Before we ask what you do with your freedom, let us turn to the life of Our Lord and Our Lady, for the supreme example of how freedom is to be used.

The First Word Our Lord is recorded as speaking in the Scripture is at the age of twelve: "I must be about my Father's business" (Lk 2:49). During His public life, He reaffirmed this dedication to His Father's will: "I always do the things that please Him" (Jn 8:29). Now on the Cross, when He goes out to meet death by freely surrendering His Life, His last words are: "Father, into your hands I commend my spirit" (Lk 23:46).

Father — Note the word of Eternal Parenthood. He did not say *Our Father* as we do, for the Father was not His and ours in the same way. He is the Natural Son of the Father; we are only the adopted sons.

Into your hands — These were the hands the prophet called "good"; the hands that guided Israel to its historical fulfillment of God's Providence; the hands that provide good things even for the birds of the air and the grass of the field.

I commend my spirit — Surrender! Consecration! Life is a cycle. We come from God and we go back again to God. Hence the purpose of living is to do God's will.

When Our Blessed Mother saw Him bow His head and deliver His Spirit, she remembered the last Word that she is recorded to have spoken in Scripture. It was to the wine steward at the marriage feast of Cana; that day when, in the language of Crashaw, "the unconscious waters saw their God and blushed." "Do whatever He tells you" (Jn 2:5).

What a beautiful valedictory! They are the most magnificent words that ever came from the lips of a woman. At the Transfiguration the Father spoke from the Heavens and said: "This is my Beloved Son... hear Him" (Mt 17:5). Now Our Blessed

Mother speaks and says, "Do His will." The sweet relationship of three decades in Nazareth now draws to a close, as Mary is about to give Emmanuel to us all. She does it by pointing out to us the one and only way of salvation: complete consecration to her Divine Son. Nowhere in the Scripture is it ever said that Mary loved her Son. Words do not prove love. True love is surrender of the will, and such is her final injunction to us: "Do whatever He tells you" (Jn 2:5).

Both the last recorded words of Jesus and those of Mary were words about freedom: a freedom *for* something. For Jesus it was the will of the Father, for Mary the will of the Son. This is the law of the universe: Nature is for man, man is for Christ, and Christ is God's.

What do you do with your freedom? You can do one of three things with it:

1. Keep it for your selfish desires.
2. Break it up into tiny little areas of trivial allegiance or passing fancy.
3. Surrender it to God.

If you keep freedom only for yourself, then, because it is arbitrary and without standards, you will find it deteriorating into a defiant self-affirmation. Once all things become allowable, simply because you desire them, you will become the slave of your choices. If your self-will decides to drink as much as you please, you soon find not only that you are no longer free not to drink, but that you belong to drink; it is your master, you are its slave. Boundless liberty is boundless tyranny. The abuse of freedom ends in the destruction of freedom. This is what Our Lord meant when He said: "Everyone who commits sin is a slave of sin" (Jn 8:34).

The second way to use freedom is to become like a humming bird, hovering first over this flower, then over that, but living for none and dying without any. In that case, you desire nothing with your whole heart, because your heart is broken into a thousand pieces. You thus become divided against yourself; a civil war rages within you; you are striking out in contradictory directions. You change your likes and desires when dissatisfied, but you never change yourself. You become very much like the man who complained to the cook at breakfast that the egg was not fresh and asked for another. She brought in an egg a minute later, but when he got to the bottom of it, he found it was the same old egg turned upside down. So it is with human nature; what has changed is the desire, not the soul.

As a result, your interest in others is not real. In your more honest moments you discover that you deal with them on the basis of self-interest; you let them speak when they agree with you, but you silence them when they disagree. Your moments of love, if you look into your soul, are nothing but a barren exchange of egotism — you talk about yourself five minutes, and your neighbor talks about himself five minutes, but if he takes longer you call him a "bore."

No wonder such people often say: "I must pull myself together." Thus do they confess that they are like broken mirrors, each reflecting a different image. In essence this is debauchery, or the inability to choose one among many attractions; the soul is diffused, multiple, or "legion," as Satan called himself. And this is the sad state of millions in the world; they are free *from* something, but free *for* nothing, because they have no purpose in life.

Finally, you can use your freedom as Our Lord did on the Cross, by surrendering His Spirit to the Father, and as Mary bade us at Cana, by doing His will in all things. This is perfect freedom: the displacement of self as the center of motivation and the fixation of our choices, decisions, and actions in the words of Our Lord: "Thy will be done on earth as it is in heaven." We are all like limpets that can live only when they cling to a rock. Our freedom forces us to adhere to something. Freedom is ours to surrender; we are free to choose our servitudes. To give that freedom to anything less than the perfect never brings ultimate peace. But to surrender to Perfect Love is to surrender to happiness and thereby be perfectly free. Thus to "serve God is to reign."

But we are afraid to give away our will. Like

St. Augustine in his early life we say: "I want to love you dear Lord, a little later on, but not now." Fearful of One who comes to us purple-robed and cypress-crowned, we ask: "Must Thy harvest fields be dunged with rotten death?" Must gold be purified by fire? Must hands that beckon bear the red livid marks of nails? Must I give up my candle, if I have the sun? Must I give up knocking if the door of love is opened? Do we not act toward God as a child who resents the affectionate embrace of his parents, because it is not our mood to love? Francis Thompson so reflected when he heard these words from the mouth of a child:

> Why do you so clasp me,
>   And draw me to your knee?
> Forsooth, you do but chafe me,
>   I pray you let me be:
> I will be loved but now and then
>   When it liketh me!
> So I heard a young child,
>   A thwart child, a young child
> Rebellious against love's arms,
>   Make its peevish cry.
> To the tender God I turn; —
>   Pardon, Love most High!
> For I think those arms were even Thine,
>   And that child even I.

There is hope for you if you are dissatisfied with your present choices, and you want the Perfect: the very void you thus create makes it possible for God to fill it. I would rather hear you say, "I am a sinner," than to hear you say, "I have no need of religion." If you admit you are a sinner, you acknowledge the need of a Redeemer; but if you have no need of religion, then you are your own god, and if you are God, I am an atheist. If you are empty, God can pour in His waters of Life; if you are filled with self, there is no room for anything else.

No man who has ever shed a sincere tear before God for the way he abused his freedom was ever lost. Even in an earthly way, have you ever noticed how much more beautiful the hills look when there are tears in your eyes? You may even see rainbows of hope. Our Lord took St. Augustine to Himself even though Augustine lamented: "Too late have I loved Thee, O Beauty ever ancient, ever new. Too late have I loved Thee."

So He will take your freedom to choose between good and evil and make it a freedom in perfection and goodness if you but surrender to that "love we fall short of in all love" and to that "Beauty that leaves all other beauty pain."

This is the week Divine Love died for you. He makes His final appeal as Love crucified. When dictators want the wills of men, they nail them to a cross.

When God wants our wills, He permits Himself to be nailed that He may never force and that we may be uncaught captives in the hands of Love.

Do you know anyone else who loves you enough to die for you?

You know your own mind, yes; but do you know your own heart? Your tears may be dried; but your heart filled? Never!

Only God can fill that. May you then give Him an hour a day in prayer and meditation always remembering that it does not require much time to make you a saint; It requires only *much love*.

EASTER

ADDRESS DELIVERED ON APRIL 1, 1945

If this second World War had not broken out, I would have found it hard to believe in God.

I do not mean the World War with its peculiar accidents of time and place and nations, but in the larger moral aspect of judgment and retribution. If nature, for example, were indifferent to infractions of its laws, if health did not decline with the refusal to eat, if blindness did not follow the plucking out of an eye, if one gathered figs from thistles, and water ran up hill, it would be difficult to believe that Supreme Intelligence had imposed order and law on the visible universe in which we live.

In like manner, if the moral order were indifferent to our infractions, if the breakdown of the nations did not follow the collapse of family life, if the affirmation that man is an animal did not make men act like animals, if the denial that God is the Author of Law did not produce a lawless and therefore a warring world, then it would be difficult to believe that God made a moral universe in which

- 141 -

men reaped where they sowed, and where the wages of sin are death.

At no time in modern history has it been easier to believe in God than now. It used to be that evil was considered a stumbling block to a belief in the Goodness of God, but today men are coming to a belief in the Goodness of God because of evil. They admit that evil today has taken on such proportions that it can be explained only by the infraction of a universal moral law that must have come from God. In a word, modern man is coming to God by way of the devil.

And such is the lesson of this Resurrection day: We come to the glory of Easter Sunday through the evil of a Good Friday; to a halo of dazzling light through the ignominy of a crown of thorns; to the dawn of a new day through the darkness of a high noon.

Calvary is only a momentary scandal. Goodness in the face of evil must suffer, for when love meets sin it will be crucified. A God who bears His Sacred Heart upon His sleeve as Our Lord did in the Incarnation, must be prepared to have daws peck at it. But at the same time, Goodness can use that suffering as the condition of overcoming evil! It can take anger and wrath and hate and say "Forgive." It can take life and offer it for another. Evil may have its hour, but God will have His day.

When therefore at one moment I see a naked

criminal on the gallows, forsaken by followers, rejected by the dominant spiritual forces of His time,
condemned by the State whose name stands in all
history as the synonym for human law; when three
days later I hear an angel say to a woman in search
of a grave, "Why are you looking among the dead
for Him Who Lives?" (Lk 24:5); when I hear Him as
the Divine Stranger on a roadway Easter afternoon
say to His companions: "Did not the Christ have
to suffer these things, and so enter into His glory?"
(Lk 24:26); when I see Him who had been nailed,
walking in the newness of life in the clouds of the
morning — then I begin to understand that since
evil could never do anything worse than crucify
Goodness, it could never be truly victorious again.
Conquered in its full armor and in the moment
of its monumental momentum, evil might in the
future win some battles, but it would always lose
the war. Evil was more powerful than goodness
when the battlefield is the physical, as a Niagara
Falls can sweep a good man to his destruction;
nevertheless, goodness is more powerful than evil
when the issue is spiritual, for as the mind of a man
can harness the destructive forces of a Niagara, so
the Goodness of God can let evil do its mightiest,
which is to crucify Divine Life and still conquer it
by rising not with wounds, but with glorious scars
on hands and feet and side.

From that day on, all the darkness in the

world cannot put out the light of a single candle. All the swords of earth cannot kill the life of a single immortal soul. All the evil in the universe cannot black out the fixed flash of that instant and intolerant enlightenment — the Lightning made eternal as the Light. No one therefore shall take away our hope for any person or nation regardless of the passing forces of evil.

Would you point to Russia then on this Easter day? I tell you that this land and this people (here I speak not of its ideology nor its present hours nor the immediate future) shall one day, not because of any present human tendencies in that direction but because of the *Christlikeness of its great souls*, hidden away from the eye of man, come to the glory of the Risen Christ. Other lands have loved Christ the Teacher, others Christ the Captain, others Christ the Truth, but here is a land whose dedication is to Christ on the Cross; the emptied Christ, the humiliated Christ, the suffering Christ.

Their long traditional concept of charity is not like ours of the Western world. We look upon salvation and redemption vertically. We live on the second floor; down in the basement there is poverty, evil and pain. We go down to the basement, bind up wounds, educate, sweep the floor and feed the hungry, and when we have done all we can, we go back again into the comforts of our second floor existence.

The Russians for centuries, on the contrary, have looked at redemption horizontally. On one side there is goodness, abundance, life; on the other side is evil, sorrow, pain. Once their great souls cross that line, the sunny side of the gap, they never go back. They go to wretchedness and evil, not to alleviate but to share, not to ease burdens but to take them on, not to do all one can and then leave, not to alleviate but to partake and to commune.

This love of participation in the sufferings of others has peopled Russia in the past and even now with the greatest spiritual underground in the world, an underground dedicated not to the destruction but the salvation of a nation, namely the 'yurodivy,' or the "born fools." He is nobody's son, nobody's father but everybody's brother. A true fool of Christ, he becomes a spectacle to men and angels, in the stark madness of absorbing the shocks of evil, by forgiving, blessing, and praying, because the love of his fellow men is stronger than his love of life.

A Russian woman who lived in close contact with these suffering unknown souls tells us the heroic Legend that the yurodivy's whisper in Russia, even this very minute. It is a variation of the old legend of St. George and the Dragon. It seems that one day St. George was about to slay the dragon, and as he drew his sword, Christ stepped in between the two, not to protect St. George, but the dragon, bidding St. George to put up his sword.

There is some suggestion here of Gethsemane, where Christ so participated in the sins of the world, that He waited until the cup of iniquity was full. Not until the chalice of the world's sin had been drained of its last drop of evil, could it be smashed and shattered without fear of spilling the dregs either on man or mother earth. So the yurodivy awaits the hour until he has filled up in his body the sufferings that are wanting to the passion of Christ, and then shall be fulfilled the vocation of Russia to bring the treasures of Christ to all the nations.

May we too learn that the burden of the world's sin is on us too, that we are responsible to some extent for the sins of all men. While earth wears wounds, we must say in Christ's name: "My Pain! My Grief! My Woe! My Tears! My Sin!"

But why should we share the burden of others? Because we love others with the love with which Christ loved us. Love everyone. Love man in sin, for to love man in sin is the only way to crush sin in man and save him. Love the lilies, for they tell us of the Father's care. Love the birds, for their song is Nature's Vespers. Love the little children, for their angels see the Face of the Father. Love families, for they are magnified trinities — Lover, the Beloved, and Love.

Love the weak, for God has chosen them to confound the strong. Love the wounded for they bear the vestigial scars of Calvary. Love the sick, for in them God's glory can be revealed. Love the ignorant, for if they know God they are the wisest of men. Love Yourself, knowing that love's greatest victory is laying siege to selfishness.

Each night as the sun goes down in the "flaming monstrance of the west," think of it as the bleeding Heart of the world, crying to you to love, for there will never be peace in the world so long as we understand VE-Day to mean Victory over Europe, but only if it means Victory over Evil through the grace and peace of Our Risen Lord and Savior Jesus Christ.